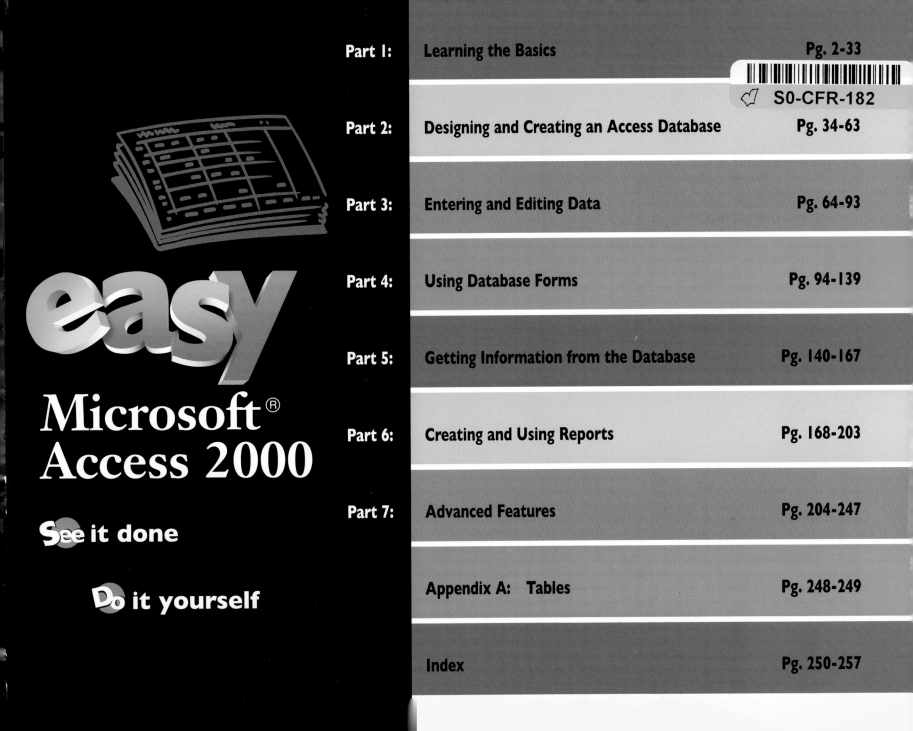

easy
Microsoft® Access 2000

See it done

Do it yourself

Part 1:	Learning the Basics	Pg. 2-33
Part 2:	Designing and Creating an Access Database	Pg. 34-63
Part 3:	Entering and Editing Data	Pg. 64-93
Part 4:	Using Database Forms	Pg. 94-139
Part 5:	Getting Information from the Database	Pg. 140-167
Part 6:	Creating and Using Reports	Pg. 168-203
Part 7:	Advanced Features	Pg. 204-247
Appendix A:	Tables	Pg. 248-249
	Index	Pg. 250-257

Part ▶ 1: Learning the Basics

1 —Installing Microsoft Access 2000
2 —Starting Access from the Start Button
3 —Opening an Existing Database
4 —Using Menu Commands
5 —Using Toolbar Buttons
6 —Using Object Buttons
7 —Selecting Objects
8 —Getting Help
9 —Navigating in Help
10 —Using Context-Sensitive Help
11 —Using the Answer Wizard
12 —Using the Index
13 —Choosing an Office Assistant
14 —Asking a Question
15 —Using Office on the Web
16 —Exiting Access

Part ▶ 2: Designing and Creating an Access Database

1 —Adding a Folder for the Database
2 —Creating a New Database
3 —Using the Table Wizard
4 —Adding a New Field in Design View
5 —Working with Number Fields
6 —Adding a Yes/No Field
7 —Saving the New Table Definition
8 —Opening a Table
9 —Changing a Field Name
10 —Moving a Field Within a Table
11 —Inserting a Field
12 —Adding a New Field in Datasheet View
13 —Deleting a Field
14 —Building a Table from Scratch

Part ▶ 3: Entering and Editing Data

1 —Entering New Information Into a Table
2 —Completing the Supplier Table
3 —Copying Information from Another Record
4 —Editing Data in a Field
5 —Undoing an Edit
6 —Searching for Information
7 —Replacing Selected Information
8 —Sorting Records
9 —Using Filters
10 —Filtering by Form
11 —Deleting a Selected Record
12 —Resizing Rows and Columns
13 —Freezing and Unfreezing Columns
14 —Hiding and Unhiding Columns

Part ▶ 4: Using Database Forms

1 —Using an AutoForm
2 —Using a Wizard to Build a Form
3 —Opening the Form Design View Window
4 —Adding Fields to a Form
5 —Moving Fields in Form Design
6 —Creating Headers and Footers
7 —Creating Labels
8 —Using a Combo Box
9 —Adding a List Box
10 —Moving Objects
11 —Editing a Label
12 —Using an Option Button
13 —Adding a Calculated Field
14 —Adding Pop-Up Tip Text to Fields
15 —Using Color in the Form
16 —Saving Your New Form
17 —Opening a Form
18 —Entering and Editing Information with a Form
19 —Changing the Field Order

Part 5: Getting Information from the Database

1 —Opening Query Design View
2 —Running and Saving a Query
3 —Adding Fields to the Query Grid
4 —Selecting Records with Wildcards
5 —Selecting Records with an OR Criteria
6 —Selecting Records with More than One Criterion
7 —Using Arithmetic Operators
8 —Adding a New Field
9 —Calculating a Value with a Query
10 —Deleting Records with a Query
11 —Creating a Query That Prompts for a Criteria Variable

Part 6: Creating and Using Reports

1 —Building a Report with a Wizard
2 —Opening the Report Design View
3 —Adding Fields to the Report
4 —Using Titles
5 —Adding Automatic Page Numbers and Dates
6 —Grouping Records
7 —Sorting Records
8 —Moving Field Labels on the Report
9 —Moving Fields on the Report
10 —Using Calculated Fields in a Report
11 —Adding Special Effects to a Report
12 —Viewing a Report
13 —Saving a Report
14 —Printing a Report

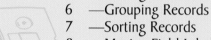

Part 7: Advanced Features

1 —Building Permanent Relationships
2 —Using a Query with Multiple Tables
3 —Creating a Report from a Query
4 —Exporting Information
5 —Importing Information
6 —Appending Data from One Table to Another
7 —Using Name AutoCorrect
8 —Viewing Data with Subdatasheets
9 —Creating Subdatasheets
10 —Creating a Data Access Page
11 —Working with Data on a Page
12 —Editing the Data Access Page Design

Copyright© 1999 by Que® Corporation

International Standard Book Number: 0-7897-1902-9

Library of Congress Catalog Card Number: 98-87614

Printed in the United States of America

First Printing: April 1999

01   00   99   4   3   2

About the Author

Jeffry Byrne has been working and teaching about computers, and particularly about database applications, for over 15 years. He is the author of numerous computer software books in several languages, including *Paradox QuickStart*, *Using CA-Simply Money*, *Easy Microsoft Access for Windows*, *Easy Microsoft Access for Windows 95*, *Easy Microsoft Access 97*, *Easy Microsoft Access 97 2nd Edition*, and now *Easy Microsoft Access 2000*. He has also contributed to *Using QuickBooks for Windows* and *Using PowerPoint 4*. In addition, he has written several other books on Microsoft SQL Server and other popular database and spreadsheet applications. When not writing about and testing software, Jeff works as a system administrator for a manufacturing company in Portland, Oregon. Jeff can be contacted at jeffbyrne@cnnw.net.

Trademarks

Warning and Disclaimer

Dedication and Acknowledgments

First and foremost, all my thanks and love go to my wife Marisa who put up with the late nights and considerable neglect so that I could finish this project. Without your belief in me I would not have come so far.

Thanks to all the people at Macmillan Computer Publishing who had a hand in this book. I know that there are many of you whom I have never talked with. Special thanks go to Neil Rowe for asking me to do the latest revision of this work, and to Matt Purcell for answering my questions and his dedication to ensuring that everything got done on time.

Executive Editor
Rosemarie Graham

Acquisitions Editor
Neil Rowe

Development Editor
Matt Purcell

Managing Editor
Jodi Jensen

Project Editor
Tonya Simpson

Indexer
Aamir Burki

Proofreader
Mona Brown

Technical Editor
Dallas Releford

Team Coordinator
Carol Ackerman

Interior Designer
Jean Bisesi

Cover Designer
Anne Jones

Illustrations
Bruce Dean

How to Use This Book

It's as Easy as 1-2-3

Each part of this book is made up of a series of short, instructional lessons, designed to help you understand basic information that you need to get the most out of your computer hardware and software.

 Click: Click the left mouse button once.

 Double-click: Click the left mouse button twice in rapid succession.

 Right-click: Click the right mouse button once.

 Pointer Arrow: Highlights an item on the screen you need to point to or focus on in the step or task.

 Selection: Highlights the area onscreen discussed in the step or task.

 Click & Type: Click once where indicated and begin typing to enter your text or data.

 Tips and ⚠ Warnings give you a heads-up for any extra information you may need while working through the task.

2 Each task includes a series of quick, easy steps designed to guide you through the procedure.

Drag

Drop

How to Drag: Point to the starting place or object. Hold down the mouse button (right or left per instructions), move the mouse to the new location, then release the button.

1 Each step is fully illustrated to show you how it looks onscreen.

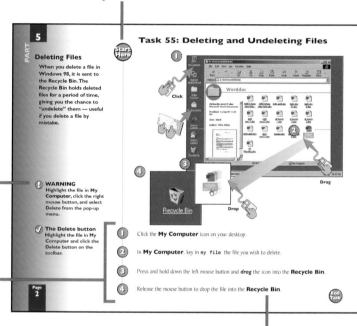

3 Items that you select or click in menus, dialog boxes, tabs, and windows are shown in **Bold**. Information you type is in a `special font`.

 Next Step: If you see this symbol, it means the task you're working on continues on the next page.

 End Task: Task is complete.

Introduction to Microsoft Access 2000

A database program is probably the most complex piece of software that you will ever use—but it doesn't have to be. You will learn to create your own database and add information to tables. Then you can build forms to view your information in a format that everyone is familiar with. In order to find information located in the database, you will create queries to ask questions and find the specific data you need. And finally, you will learn to print reports from the information in the database.

Access 2000 is more than a simple facelift from earlier versions. Much is new here, and although there is much for you to learn in using Access 2000, this book will lead you step by step through the process. Each task throughout this book shows you specifically how to accomplish the necessary job in the simplest way.

You can easily use this book as a simple reference or read it from start to finish, working along with each task as you go. Whichever way you prefer, *Easy Microsoft Access 2000* shows you how it is done and how you can do it yourself.

Tell Us What You Think!

As the reader of this book, *you* are our most important critic and commentator. We value your opinion and want to know what we're doing right, what we could do better, what areas you'd like to see us publish in, and any other words of wisdom you're willing to pass our way.

As the Executive Editor for the Database team at Macmillan Computer Publishing, I welcome your comments. You can fax, email, or write me directly to let me know what you did or didn't like about this book—as well as what we can do to make our books stronger.

Please note that I cannot help you with technical problems related to the topic of this book, and that due to the high volume of mail I receive, I might not be able to reply to every message.

When you write, please be sure to include this book's title and author as well as your name and phone or fax number. I will carefully review your comments and share them with the author and editors who worked on the book.

Fax: 317-817-7070

Email: databases@mcp.com

Mail: Rosemarie Graham
          Executive Editor
          Database Team
          Macmillan Computer Publishing
          201 West 103rd Street
          Indianapolis, IN 46290 USA

Learning the Basics

This section introduces you to the new look and feel of Microsoft Access 2000. You will learn to start and exit the program and use the various help options. Most of the tasks that you will work with in this part can be accomplished using your mouse, with minimal keyboarding required. The simplest method is shown as you use each task. Some alternative methods for doing a task are mentioned in the tips included throughout the book.

In this part of *Easy Microsoft Access 2000*, you learn to open an Access database file, select menu commands, and use the toolbar. You also learn how to use the help systems, including the Office Assistant. If you are already familiar with Windows 95 or Windows 98 (you know how to open and exit programs and use Windows 95–style menus), you can skip ahead to Task 6. If you are not familiar with these topics, then be sure to work through them carefully. These tasks are applicable to almost any of the other Windows-type applications you might use.

Although you can use most of the Access features using either the mouse or the keyboard, many functions are easier when you use the mouse, and some are accessible only with a mouse. As of this writing, you can input information into a field only by keyboarding; the keyboard will remain the primary input method for text until mice learn to type or voice input becomes a workable reality.

Tasks

Task #		Page #
1	Installing Microsoft Access 2000	4
2	Starting Access from the Start Button	8
3	Opening an Existing Database	10
4	Using Menu Commands	14
5	Using Toolbar Buttons	16
6	Using Object Buttons	17
7	Selecting Objects	18
8	Getting Help	20
9	Navigating in Help	22
10	Using Context-Sensitive Help	23
11	Using the Answer Wizard	24
12	Using the Index	26
13	Choosing an Office Assistant	28
14	Asking a Question	30
15	Using Office on the Web	32
16	Exiting Access	33

Task 1: Installing Microsoft Access 2000

Before you can begin to use Access, you must install the program. If you are working at a company with some type of an information systems department, someone else probably will install the program for you. If this isn't the case, then you will simply install the program yourself.

First, make sure you have the Microsoft Access CD-ROM and the CD key number handy. This task assumes that you are using the Microsoft Office Professional on CD-ROM. The CD key will be located on a label on the back of the CD-ROM's jewel case.

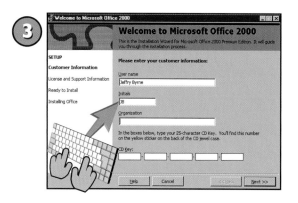
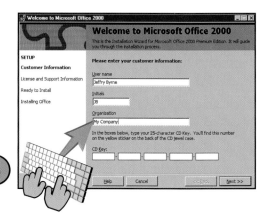

 ✓ **The Setup Program**
If the installation program does not autostart for you, browse the CD-ROM in Windows Explorer. Double-click SETUP.EXE. This is the name of the setup program that will install your application.

 Insert the CD-ROM with the Access program into your CD-ROM drive, and soon the installation routine will start. Wait for the user information Welcome screen to be displayed.

 In the **User Name** text box, type your name, and then press the Tab key to move to the next text box.

 Type your initials in the second text box, and then press the Tab key again.

Type your company name, if applicable, and press the Tab key once more.

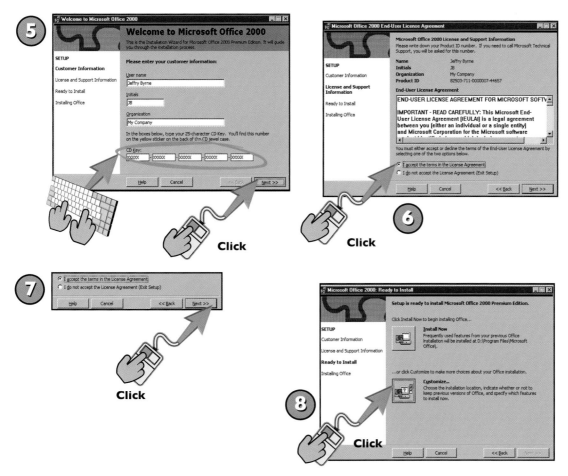

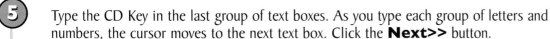

5 Type the CD Key in the last group of text boxes. As you type each group of letters and numbers, the cursor moves to the next text box. Click the **Next>>** button.

6 To install Access or Office 2000, click the **I accept the terms in the License Agreement** option button. You can't install the program without accepting the license.

7 Click the **Next>>** button to move to the next dialog box.

8 Click the **Customize** button to select the specific components to be installed. You can always add additional components later.

✅ **Different Buttons Names?**
If you are upgrading a Microsoft Office 97 installation, you would see an **Upgrade Now** button in place of the **Install Now** button.

Installing Microsoft Access 2000 Continued

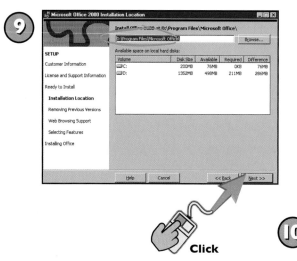

 Installation Icons
Items shown with a computer icon mean that they will be installed now, while those with the number 1 on them will be installed the first time they are accessed. A CD icon means that it can be run with the installation CD in the CD-ROM drive. An X means it is not available, and you must run the setup program again to install it.

 Choose the location where the application will be installed. The default location will normally be fine. Click the **Next>>** button.

 The primary program components are always installed. Click the **+** (plus sign) beside **Microsoft Access for Windows**.

The items displayed with a little **1** on their icon will be installed the first time you use them. Click the **+** beside **Sample Databases**, displaying the sample databases.

Click

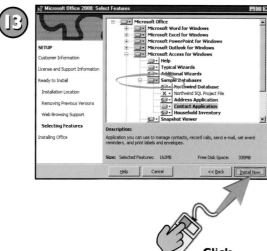

Click

12. Click **Contact Application**, and select the **Run from My Computer** option from the menu.

13. The **1** is removed from the icon. Click the **Install Now** button to begin. When installation is complete, you are prompted to reboot your system to complete the process.

End
Task

Task 2: Starting Access from the Start Button

Access is a database program that works only in the Windows 95, Windows 98, or Windows NT 4 environment. After you install Access on your computer system, you can start the program from the **Start** button, located on the taskbar at the bottom of your screen. If your taskbar is not visible, drag the mouse to the bottom of your screen and see if the taskbar pops up. It might also be located at one of the other edges of your screen.

The Windows taskbar **Start** button opens a series of menus that enable you to open and work with most of the programs and applications installed on your computer. Here you will use the **Start** button menus to open Access.

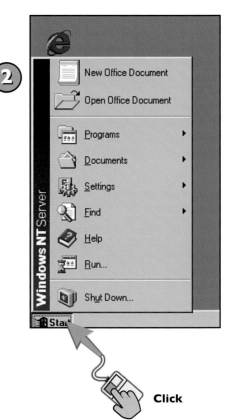

Click

When you place the mouse pointer on the **Start** button, notice the ToolTip that says **Click here to begin** floating above the button.

Click the **Start** button, displaying the menu. Note that your own menu structure might be different than this example.

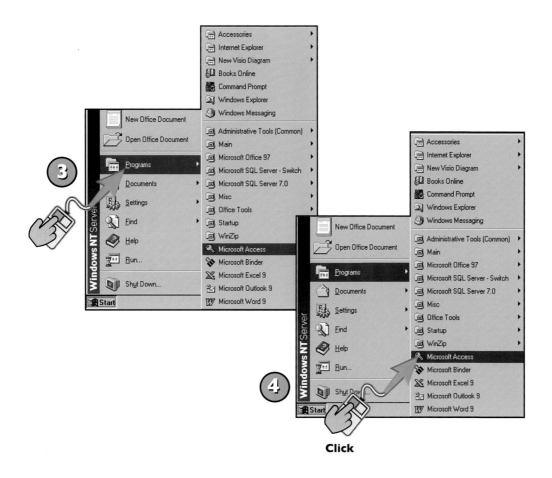

Click

<table>
<tr>
<td>3</td>
<td>Move the mouse up to the **Programs** option and display its submenu.</td>
</tr>
<tr>
<td>4</td>
<td>Click the **Microsoft Access** option on this submenu to open the Access application.</td>
</tr>
</table>

Task 3: Opening an Existing Database

In this task you learn to select a database file and then open it. In this task you use the sample database named **Contact Application** that you installed in Task 1. Remember that this database is not normally installed along with the program. In order to add data to a database file, you first must locate the file on your disk and then open it inside the **Access** application. When you open a database file, you gain access to the information located in the tables.

Start Here

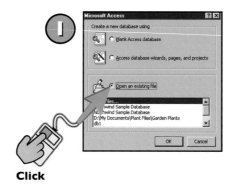
Click

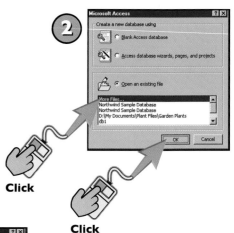
Click

Click

Click

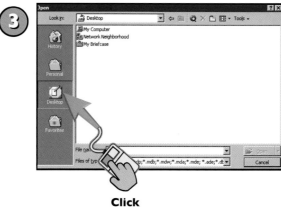
Click

1. Select **Open an Existing File** by clicking inside the option button circle. The black dot inside the circle means the option has been selected.

2. Click **More Files** inside the list box, and then click the **OK** button to select the file to be opened.

3. Access starts searching for more files in your Personal folder. Click the **Desktop** button on the button bar on the left, moving to the top level to begin your search.

Next Step

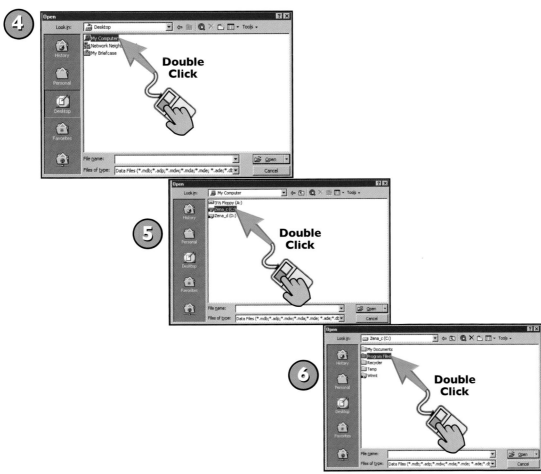

(4) Find the **Contacts** database by double-clicking **My Computer**.

(5) Double-click on **C**. You might need to select a different letter if you have installed Access on a drive other than C. Your drives might not have a name associated with them.

(6) Double-click **Program Files**.

Next Step

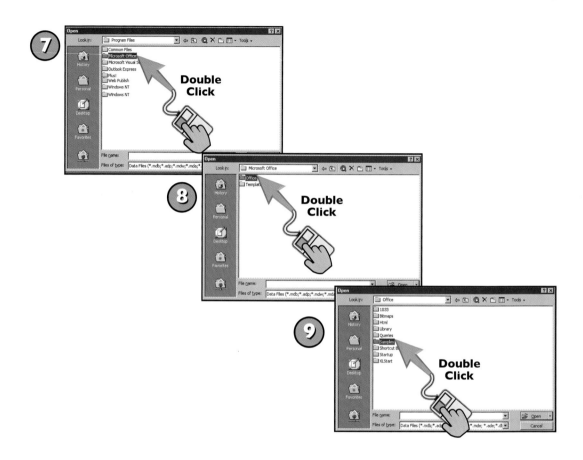

7 Double-click **Microsoft Office**. This is the default location for the Office 2000 applications.

8 Double-click the **Office** folder.

9 Double-click the **Samples** folder. If you installed Access in a different folder, make the necessary changes to your selections.

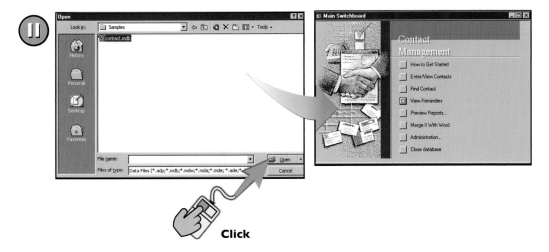

10 Click **contact.mdb** to select it.

11 Click the **Open** button. After a few moments the Contacts database will open.

Task 4: Using Menu Commands

You access the menu commands through the menu bar at the top of the screen. Some commands and functions are accessed through a series of menus, submenus, or dialog boxes. Unlike a menu, a dialog box often enables you to make several choices about the object you are working with, and then apply all the selections at once. You can select menu commands and many options available in dialog boxes by using either the keyboard or the mouse. When available, a shortcut keyboard combination is displayed to the right of the command on the menu, such as **Ctrl+P** to print an item.

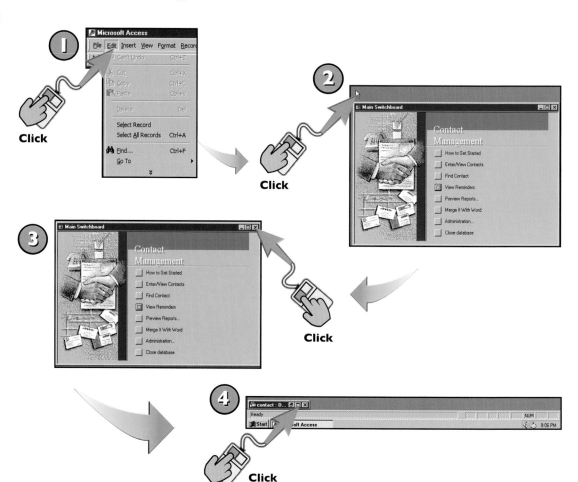

Start Here

Click

Click

Click

Click

① Click the mouse on the **Edit** option on the menu bar to display its menu.

② Now move the mouse away from the menu to a blank area on the Access desktop and click to deselect the menu.

③ Click the Close (**X**) button on the Main Switchboard form to close it.

④ Click the Restore button on the minimized Contact database window.

Next Step

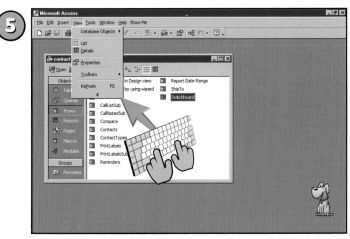

Alt + V

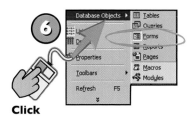

Click

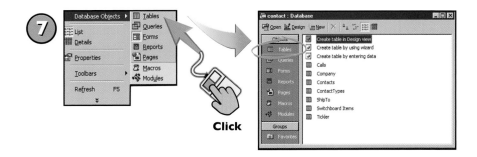

Click

5 Press the Alt key on your keyboard to activate the menu, and then press the letter V to display the **View** menu.

6 Click the **Database Objects** option to display its submenu, the list of the Access object groups. The currently selected object (**Forms**) has a depressed button beside its name.

7 Click the **Tables** menu option, and see how the Database window changes from the **Forms** group to the **Tables** group.

✓ **Keyboard Shortcuts**
To the right of some menu items you will see a two-key keyboard shortcut option. You can access these menu options without going through the menus by pressing the **Ctrl** key and then the indicated letter at the same time. Menu items that are dimmed are not available.

✓ **More Shortcuts**
Any time you see an underlined letter on a menu option, it is the hotkey. The menu item can be immediately accessed through the hotkey by holding down both the **Alt** key and the underlined letter on your keyboard.

End Task

Task 5: Using Toolbar Buttons

Many commands and functions are only a single mouse click away on your toolbar, but not all commands are available. As you work with different objects, Access might add secondary toolbars to your screen, giving you access to more options.

Access places a primary toolbar beneath the menu and a secondary toolbar on the Database window. The primary toolbar contains buttons used for general purposes, whereas the secondary toolbar has buttons particular to the database window and the current object.

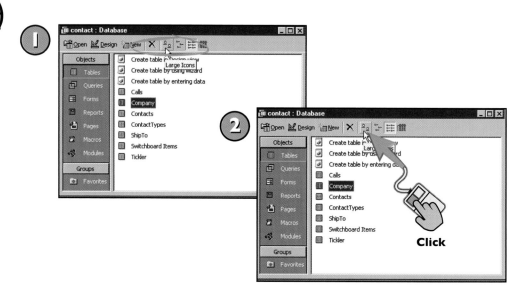

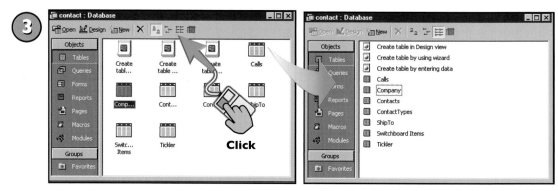

① Move the mouse pointer so that it is on the Large Icons button, and pause it there. A small ToolTip displays to explain the use for the button.

② Click the button, and all the objects in the Tables window change to large icons.

③ Click the List toolbar button to change the icons back to the default List format.

Task 6: Using Object Buttons

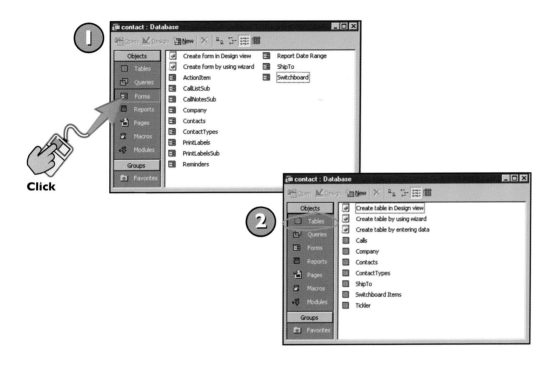

Click

On the left side of the Database window is a series of seven object buttons. These are used to gain access to the major object categories: Tables, Queries, Forms, Reports, Pages, Macros, and Modules. The simplest way to work with these object buttons is to use the mouse.

 Click the **Forms** object button. See how the objects displayed in the list box change.

 Press the Tab key once to activate the object buttons. Press the up or down arrow keys to select a button, and then press Enter to select it. Here the Tables object has been selected.

✔ Choosing Object Buttons

If you accidentally click the wrong object button, just select another. Notice how the button appears to be raised when the mouse pointer is on it. The raised button is the one that would be selected if you clicked then.

Task 7: Selecting Objects

Start Here

object list is a listing of
roup of specific object
pes. After you have
isplayed them, what do
you do with them? Each
different object type
performs specific jobs. For
example, tables are used to
store information, and
reports are used to print
the information in a specific
format.

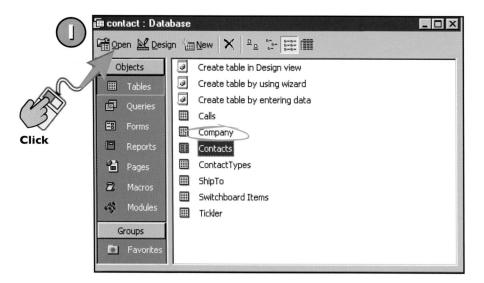

Click

Click

① Select the **Company** table, and then click the **Open** button on the Database toolbar. The Company table opens on your screen.

② Click the Close (**X**) button on the table window.

Next Step

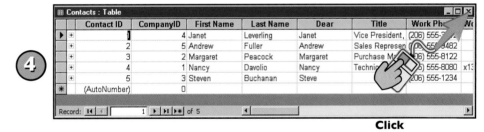

3. Double-click the **Contacts** table.

4. The Contacts table opens. Click the Close (**X**) button on the table window to close the table.

Task 8: Getting Help

Start Here

Access provides several avenues to get the help you might need on its many features. In earlier days, you would have received a large manual to go with your program; now help is limited to various help screens and methods. Access has a very comprehensive online help that makes it easy to find the information you are looking for. From within the Access Help system, you can choose from three major venues: a **Contents** section, an index, and the **Answer Wizard** system. Here you will use the Contents help.

Click

Click

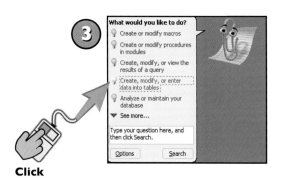

Click

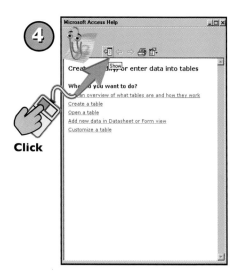

Click

---

1 From within Access, click the **Help** menu option to display the Help menu.

2 Click the **Microsoft Access Help** option to display the Office Assistant.

3 Click the light bulb button beside **Create, modify, or enter data into tables** in the dialog balloon. The help window displayed beside Access itself is a new feature.

4 Click the Show button on the Help toolbar. This will display an additional pane to the Help system.

Next Step

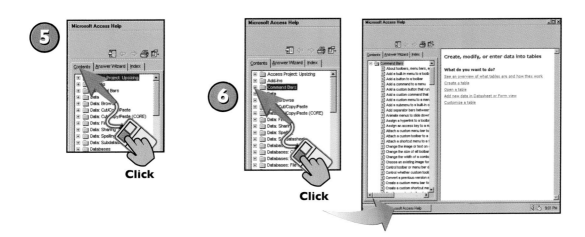

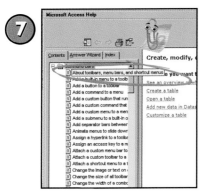

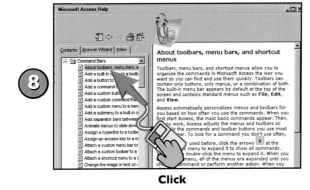

5 If the **Contents** tab button is not already selected, click it to display the Contents list.

6 Click the **+** (plus sign) beside the **Command Bars** option. A new list of topics displays.

7 Place the mouse pointer on the first option. Access displays the entire topic title, even though it is too long to fit within the list box.

8 Click the topic **About toolbars, menu bars, and shortcut menus**. The help text for the selected topic displays in the right window.

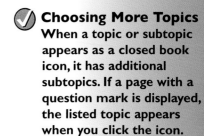

✓ **Choosing More Topics**
When a topic or subtopic appears as a closed book icon, it has additional subtopics. If a page with a question mark is displayed, the listed topic appears when you click the icon.

Task 9: Navigating in Help

The new Access 2000 Help uses a navigation format that is very much like a Web browser. The Help texts extensively use hyperlinks to jump you to other help pages, and **Back** and **Forward** buttons to either go back to a previously viewed page or move forward to the next page in a series. Hyperlinks are displayed as blue underlined text. If you click on one of these to view its underlying page, and then return to the page, the hyperlink text changes from blue to purple (assuming you are using the normal Windows screen colors). This task continues from the previous one.

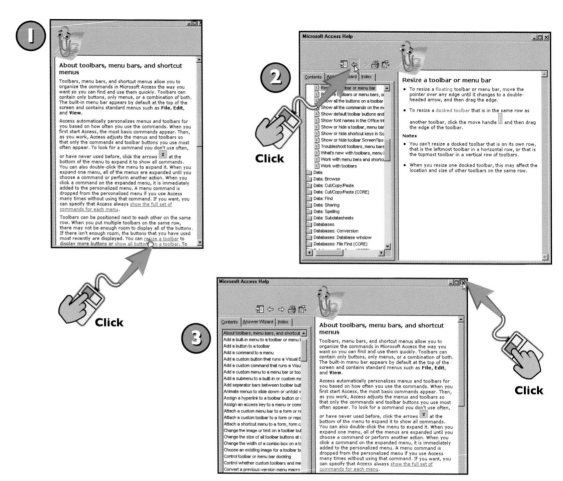

Click

Click

Click

Click

 Click on the hyperlink **resize a toolbar**. Notice how the mouse pointer changes shape to resemble a hand with a pointing finger.

 Click the Back button to return to the previous help.

 Click the Close (**X**) button on the Help window to return to the Access window.

Task 10: Using Context-Sensitive Help

Start Here

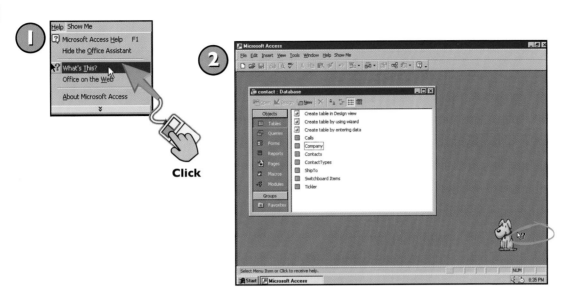

Click

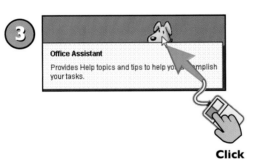

Click

In addition to finding help by subjects and selected words, you can also get help relative to the specific task you are currently performing or on a selected object. This type of help is called *context-sensitive*. For example, if you aren't sure what a specific object does, such as a toolbar button, or you simply want a better definition than a ToolTip, using the context-sensitive help option will display a pop-up definition of the selected object.

① Select the **Help** menu on the menu bar, and then click the **What's This?** option from the drop-down menu list.

② Move the mouse pointer, which has changed shape to an arrow with a question mark, onto the Office Assistant.

③ Click on the Office Assistant, and the pop-up definition box displays.

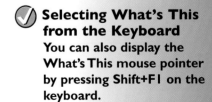

Selecting What's This from the Keyboard
You can also display the What's This mouse pointer by pressing Shift+F1 on the keyboard.

End Task

Task 11: Using the Answer Wizard

The Answer Wizard is an alternative to using the Office Assistant. You can enter a short description of what you want to do or know more about, and the Answer Wizard will display the options that it believes match your request. You can then choose from the list a topic that best fits your needs, or reword the description and try again.

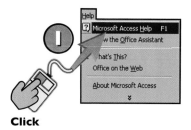

Click

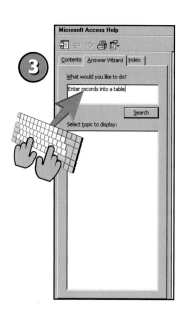

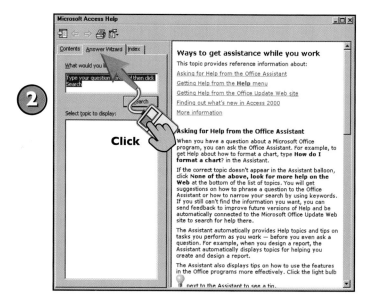

Click

(1) Click the **Help** option on the menu bar, and select **Microsoft Access Help** from the menu.

(2) Expand the Help window by clicking the Show button, and then click the **Answer Wizard** tab button.

(3) In the **What would you like to do?** text box, type what you want more information on. For example, type **Enter records into a table**.

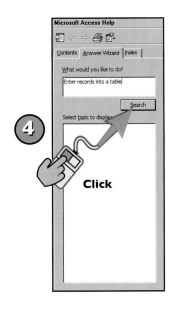

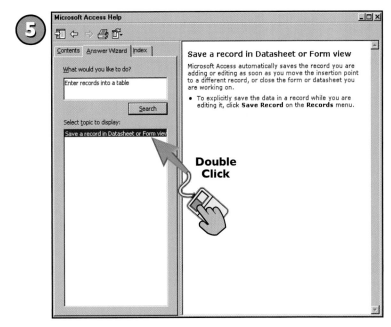

4 Click **Search**. The first topic displays on the right.

5 Double-click on **Save a record...** to display the topic.

Searching for a Different Topic
You can search for other topics of interest simply by typing over the entry you made in step 3, and then clicking the **Search** button again.

Task 12: Using the Index

The Access index is an excellent method of searching for help on a specific topic. The index works like an index in a book, but easier. With the index, you simply type a word or phrase or select from a list of key words, and Access shows you a list of topics that relate to the item you entered. After you select one of the topics displayed in the list, help for the selected topic appears in the right window pane. The index help uses the same navigation techniques as the rest of Help does. This task continues from the previous task, or you will need to open Help.

✔ Using the Help Window

If you are already using one form of Help, such as the Answer Wizard, you don't have to close that window and restart it simply to use the index or view the contents Help.

Start Here

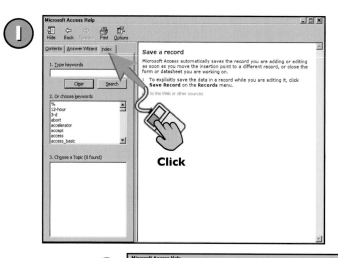

Click

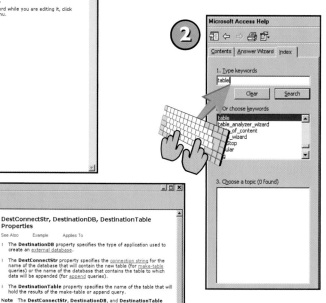

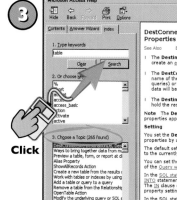

Click

Click the **Index** tab button in the Help window.

Use the index to get help on specific topics by typing a word in the upper text box. Type **table** and see the list of keywords change.

Click the **Search** button. A list of topics displays in the lower of the three list boxes. In this case, 265 topics were found.

Next Step

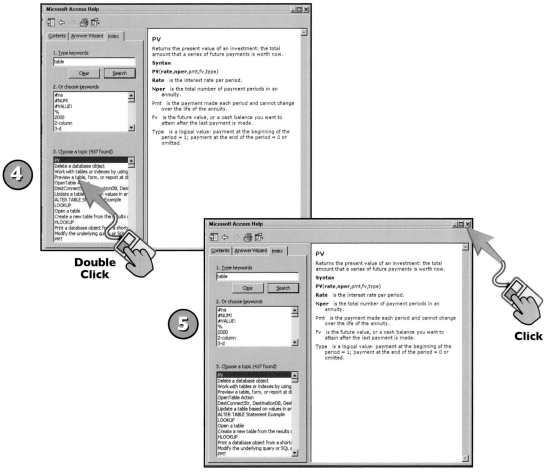

Double Click

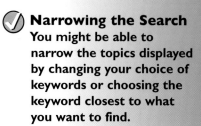

Click

4 Click the topic that is closest to what you want help on. For example, double-click the fourth option **Preview a table, form, or report at...**.

5 Click the Close (**X**) button on the Help window to return to the main Access window.

✓ **Narrowing the Search**
You might be able to narrow the topics displayed by changing your choice of keywords or choosing the keyword closest to what you want to find.

Task 13: Choosing an Office Assistant

The Office Assistant is a new form of interactive help. You may choose from among several unique assistants and set many different options, such as sounds and animation. They can be activated when you press the F1 key or click the assistant. You can search for and display several topics that might help you answer your question.

The assistant also watches what you are doing and offers to help you perform new tasks if it sees that you are working harder than you need to on a specific task. The assistant can also show daily tips that change each time you start Access, or you can view and cycle through them as needed.

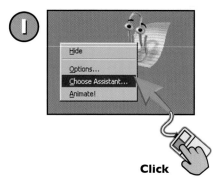

Click

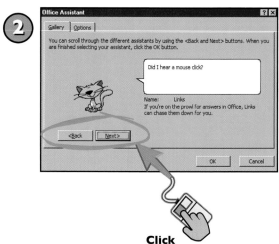

Click

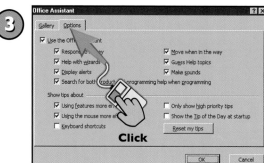

Click

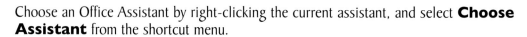

① Choose an Office Assistant by right-clicking the current assistant, and select **Choose Assistant** from the shortcut menu.

② Click the **<Back** or **Next>** buttons to cycle through the various assistants, and then stop on the Office Assistant that you want to select.

③ Each assistant displays some of its characteristics for you as you view it. Click the **Options** tab when you have made your choice.

Next Step

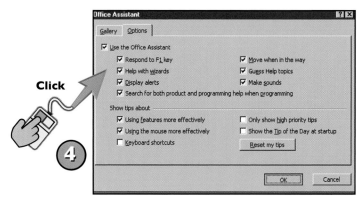

Click

④

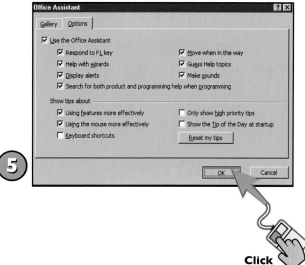

⑤

Click

④ You use the **Options** tab selections to customize your assistant; simply check or uncheck the various check boxes.

⑤ Click **OK** after you have made all your selections. This closes the Office Assistant dialog box and sets your assistant if you made any changes.

Task 14: Asking a Question

To use the interactive **Office Assistant**, you must ask it a question. It then searches through all the Access help topics and displays a selection of topics that might bring you the answer for which you are searching. The answers are shown in a dialog balloon, and when selected display the help topic for that selection.

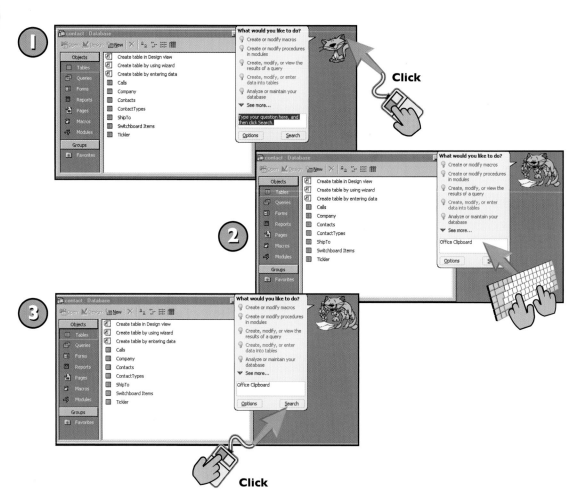

Click

Click

Start Here

 Click the Office Assistant, and the dialog balloon displays next to it.

 Type **Office Clipboard** into the text box, or anything else that you want more information about.

 Click the **Search** button to start the assistant searching for information.

✅ **Seeing More Help Topics**

If none of the topics shown in the dialog balloon appear to be what you want, click the **See more** option to view more help topics. You can also try rewording your request and then clicking the **Search** button again.

Next Step

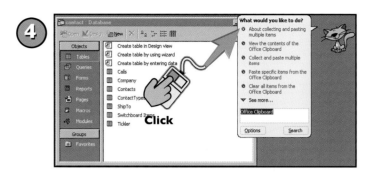

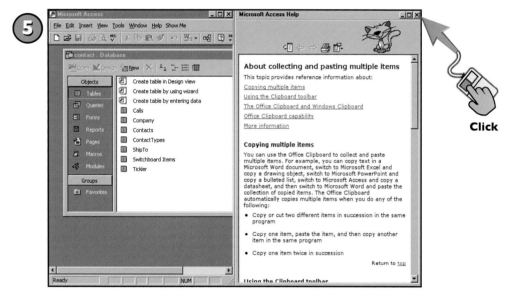

4 Click the blue button beside the **About collecting and pasting multiple items** option to view the help dialog on this specific topic.

5 Click the Close (**X**) button at the upper-right corner of the help dialog box to close it and return to the Access desktop.

Task 15: Using Office on the Web

Start
Here

This is a new form of help to Access and the rest of Microsoft Office. If you can't find what you need in any other form of help, you can directly access Microsoft's Web site for Office products. In order to use this type of help, you must have some form of an Internet connection that enables you to view Web pages, and Microsoft Internet Explorer 5.0 or later.

Click

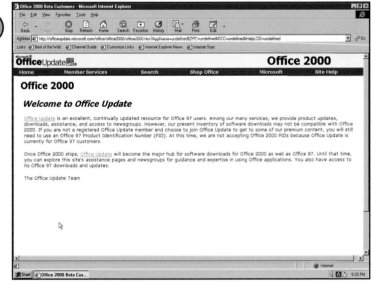

(1) Click **Help** and then **Office on the Web** from the menu bar.

(2) Microsoft Internet Explorer will open and connect to Microsoft's Office on the Web site.

End
Task

Task 16: Exiting Access

Start Here

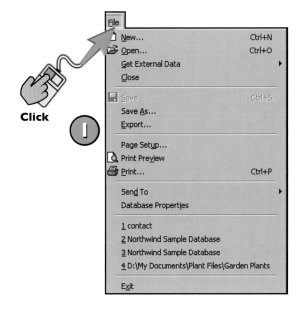

Click

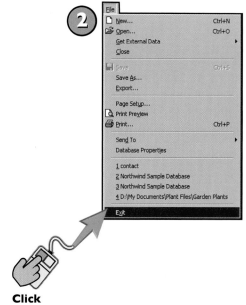

Click

After you have completed your tasks in **Access**, or any time you leave your computer for some time, such as at the end of the day, you should properly exit from the program. If a power or hardware failure occurs, your chances of successful information recovery increase.

✔ **Using the Close Button**
You can also exit from Access by clicking the Close button (**X**) in the upper-right corner of the program window or by pressing the Alt+F4 key combination.

✔ **Escaping From a Menu**
If, after opening the **File** menu, you decide you are not ready to exit Access, press the Esc key to back out of the menu. You can also click the mouse anywhere on the desktop to close the menu.

1 Open the **File** menu, displaying the drop-down menu list.

2 Click the **Exit** command on the **File** menu, and Access will shut down and return you to the Windows desktop.

End Task

PART 2

Designing and Creating an Access Database

When you design an Access database, you must understand all the components of one. All information is stored in a table, and each table contains information about a particular thing: customers, products, orders, and so on. A table is composed of rows and columns—the rows contain *records* and columns are *fields*. There is one record for each item in the table. Every record is divided into fields, and every record in a table uses the same fields. A field contains a distinct piece of information about the record.

The goal of the relational database is to remove as much duplicate information as possible. Each table has information about one thing: customers, products, and so on. The records in a table are then related to the records in another table through a primary and foreign key relationship. The following figure shows how the primary key CustomerID in a Customers table relates to a foreign key CustomerID in an Invoice table.

Tasks

Task #		Page #
1	Adding a Folder for the Database	36
2	Creating a New Database	38
3	Using the Table Wizard	40
4	Adding a New Field in Design View	44
5	Working with Number Fields	46
6	Adding a Yes/No Field	48
7	Saving the New Table Definition	50
8	Opening a Table	51
9	Changing a Field Name	52
10	Moving a Field Within a Table	54
11	Inserting a Field	56
12	Adding a New Field in Datasheet View	58
13	Deleting a Field	59
14	Building a Table from Scratch	60

Task 1: Adding a Folder for the Database

When you create a new database, you must place it in a folder. You can add the new database file to whichever default folder Access selects, but you probably will want to choose your own folder. It is highly recommended that you create a new folder for your Access databases. You can place each database into its own folder or group them according to types. Just be consistent in your choice.

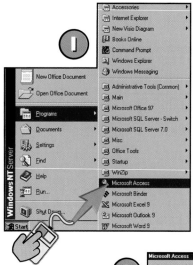

Click

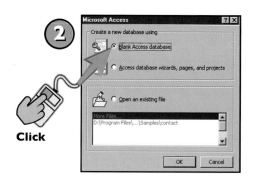

Click

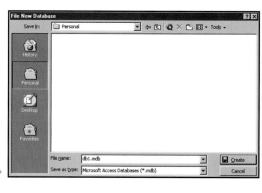

Click

(1) Start Access by clicking the **Start** button, **Programs**, **Microsoft Access**.

(2) Click the **Blank Access Database** option button.

(3) Click **OK**, opening the File New Database dialog box.

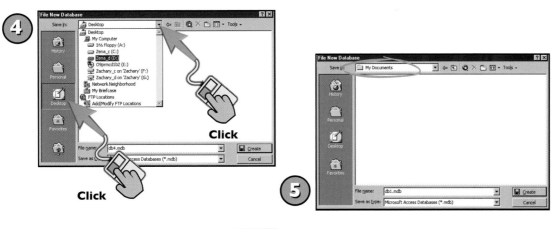

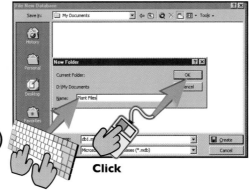

4 Click the **Desktop** button, and then select the down arrow next to the **Desktop** listing in the **Save in:** box.

5 Drill down to the **My Documents** folder.

6 Click the Create New Folder button to display the New Folder dialog box.

7 In the **Name** text box, type **Plant Files**, and then click the **OK** button to create the new folder.

Task 2: Creating a New Database

This task continues from Task 1. After you have created the folder in which you will place your new database, you must name the database. Unlike most programs, you must name the database and then create it.

Access automatically uses the name *db1* for your database. Unless you plan to create a single database, you will want to use a descriptive name. The name you give is limited to 255 characters and can include spaces and most other characters. You cannot use leading spaces, periods, exclamation points, the back-quote character, or square brackets.

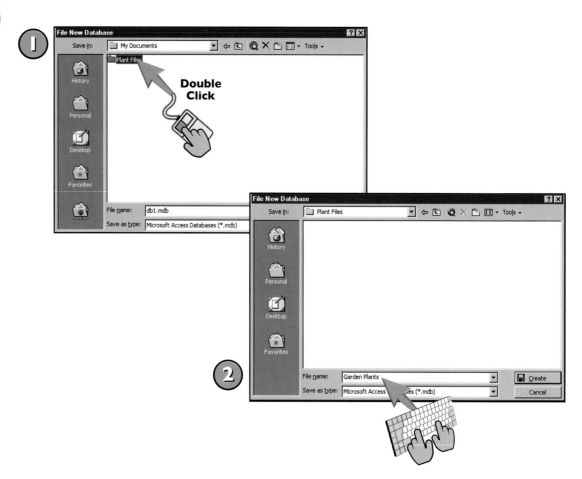

Open the folder by double-clicking the **Plant Files** folder in the list box.

Press the Tab key once to select the old filename, and then type **Garden Plants** in its place.

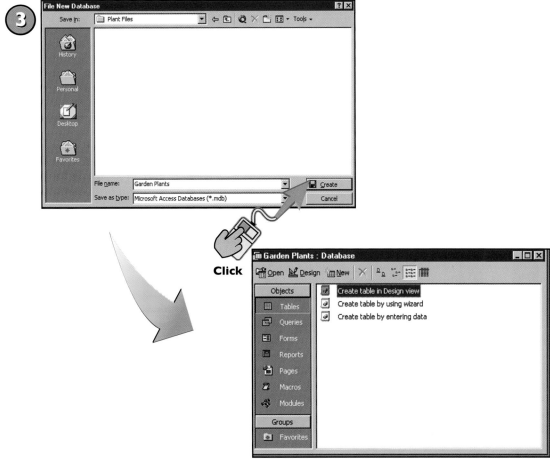

Click

③ Click the **Create** button. Access creates and opens the new database.

Task 3: Using the Table Wizard

In Task 2 you created the file or document in which you will place your database and its tables, forms, and other objects. You have available a special helper called the Table Wizard that you can use to create many types of tables.

You will see a series of dialog boxes, and you simply fill in the necessary information or choose different options. When you are finished, you will have a new table.

Click

Double Click

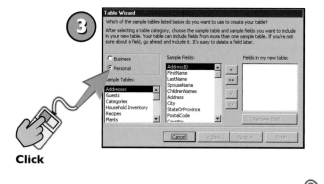

Click

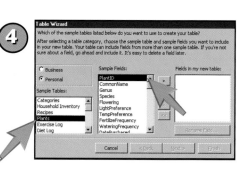

Click

✓ **Using Samples**
Scroll up and down the Sample Tables list box to view the various available tables. Be sure to check out both the Personal and Business lists.

1. Click the **Tables** object button.

2. Double-click **Create table by using wizard** in the database window to start the wizard.

3. Click the **Personal** option button, and Access will display the list of personal categories of tables in the **Sample Tables** list box.

4. Select the **Plants** table by scrolling down the **Sample Tables** list box. Notice the new list of predefined fields in the next list box.

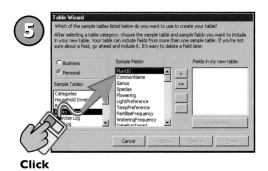

Click

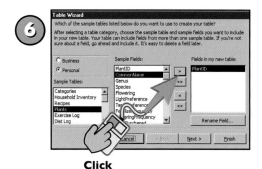

Click

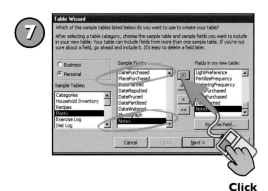

Click

---

5 Click the **PlantID** field in the **Sample Fields** list box as the first field to be included in the new table.

6 Click the **>** button, and Access will copy the selected field to the list box on the right, where it will be included in the new table.

7 Select these fields and click the **>** button to add them to the list: **CommonName**, **Genus**, **Species**, **Flowering**, **LightPreference**, **FertilizeFrequency**, **WateringFrequency**, **DatePurchased**, **PlacePurchased**, **DatePlanted**, and **Notes**.

Other Fields
If the **Sample Fields** list box doesn't include a field that you want for the table, don't worry. You can add the new field later.

Using the Table Wizard Continued

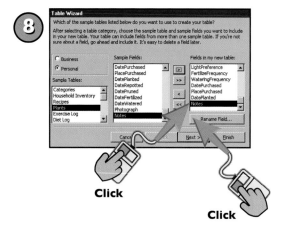

Click

Click

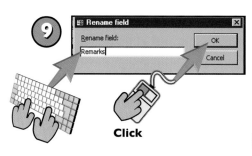

Click

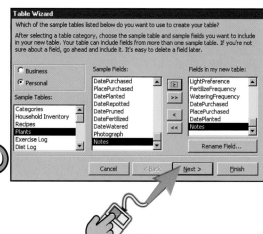

Click

(8) Select the **Notes** field and click the **Rename Field** button.

(9) Type **Remarks** into the text box and click **OK**.

(10) Click the **Next>** button.

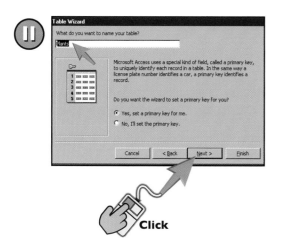

Click

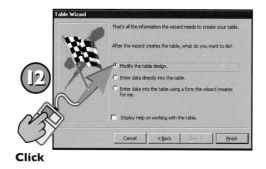

Click

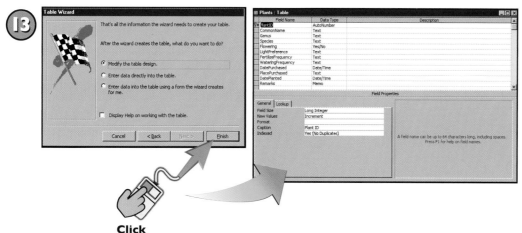

Click

11 Here you enter a name for the database and allow Access to set a primary key. The default options will work. Click the **Next>** button. This is the final wizard dialog box.

12 Click the **Modify the table design** option button.

13 Click the **Finish** button. Access completes the table and opens it in the Design View window.

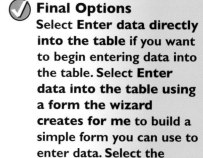

Final Options
Select **Enter data directly into the table** if you want to begin entering data into the table. Select **Enter data into the table using a form the wizard creates for me** to build a simple form you can use to enter data. Select the **Display Help...** check box at the bottom to get help from the **Office Assistant**.

Task 4: Adding a New Field in Design View

Start Here

This task continues from the previous task. When you use the various wizards, you sometimes will want to make changes to the default settings. In the Plants table example, the predefined table does not have a field for the color of a flower.

To add a field to the table you must use the Design view option and add the field yourself. When adding a new field, you must provide a field name, a data type, and some formatting information.

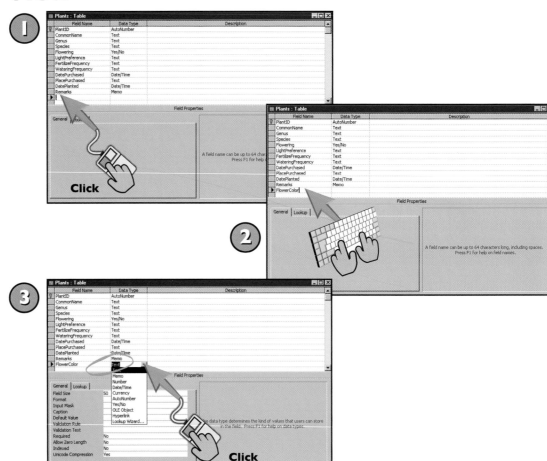

1. Click the mouse pointer in the first empty row in the **Field Name** column, just below the field named **Remarks**.

2. Type **FlowerColor** into the empty space.

3. Press the Tab key to move to the **Data Type** column, and select **Text** as the data type. Click the down-arrow button to see the other data types available on the drop-down menu.

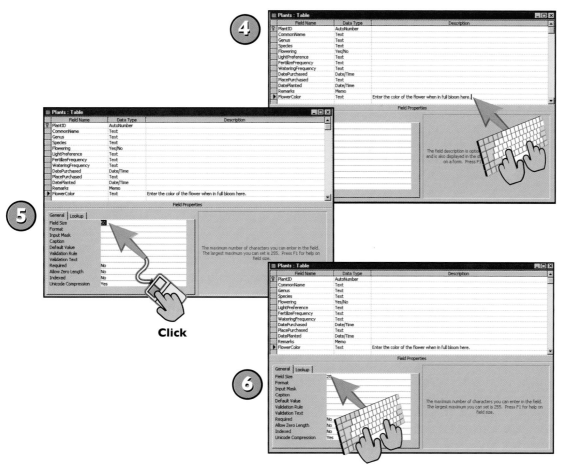

Click

④ Press the Tab key to move to the **Description** column and type `Enter the color of the flower when in full bloom here`.

⑤ Press the F6 key to switch to the lower pane of the window. You can also just click the **Field Size** option.

⑥ Type **20** as the new field size for this column.

✓ **Using Descriptions**
The note you type into the **Description** column will be displayed on the status bar when you enter the column in a table or form view.

✓ **Choosing a Field Length**
The maximum length for a text field is 255 characters and a default of 50. Don't arbitrarily set the length to 255. This length is used to allocate drive space and memory storage. Set this to a realistic size for the data.

Task 5: Working with Number Fields

Number information is often used in databases. Numeric data includes things like quantities, pricing, cost data, temperature, and any other information stored as numbers. Access provides several special data types to handle number information only.

When you store number information in a numeric field, you can use that data in calculations. For example, you can multiply the price of an item by the number of items purchased and get the extended price. Calculated values are not normally stored in a database because they take up unnecessary disk space.

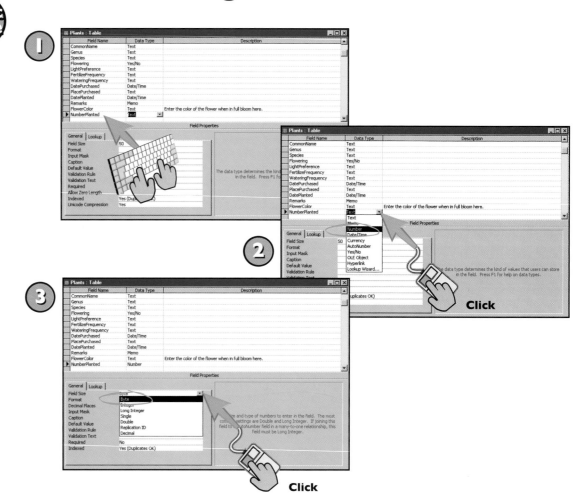

Start Here

Need Help Choosing a Field Size?

The Byte data type enables you to enter any positive, whole number between 0 and 255. For help with the Field Size property press the F1 key.

1 After completing Task 4, click in the blank row under **FlowerColor** and type **NumberPlanted**. Press the Tab key.

2 Click the button in the **Data Type** column and select **Number** from the drop-down list for this field.

3 Press F6, or click in the text box beside **Field Size**, and click the button to display the option list. Select the **Byte** option.

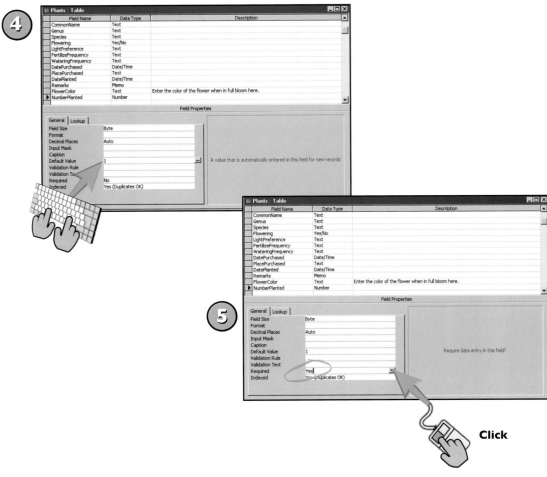

Click

Click the **Default Value** text box and type **1**. This number will automatically be entered into the field when you create a new record, but can be overwritten.

Move down to the **Required** text box, click the arrow button, and select **Yes**. This means that a value must be entered into this field, even if it is only a zero.

✅ **Using Date/Time Fields**
For fields used for date or time information, select the Date/Time data type. A date field can hold any date from January 1, 100 to December 31, 9999.

Task 6: Adding a Yes/No Field

In some tables you will want to save data that can be a simple Yes or No answer. Instead of having to type Yes or No for every record, you can use the Yes/No data type.
Any field needing a Yes/No, True/False, or On/Off response can use this data type. The Yes/No data type can be represented in a table or form with a text box, a check box, or a drop-down list. This can also help you eliminate data entry errors by allowing the user to select only one of two valid responses.

Start Here

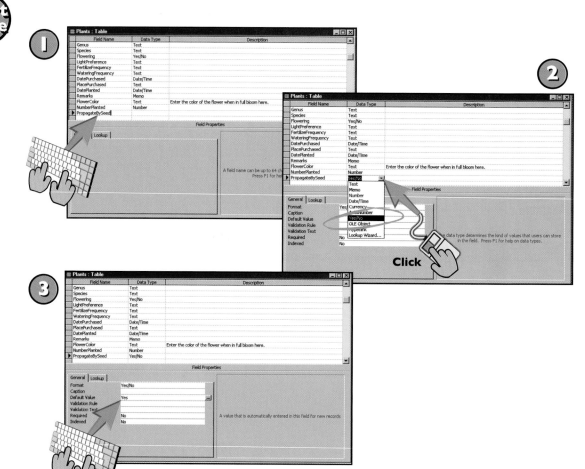

✓ Shortcut to Data Types

If you know the name of the data type you want, type the first letter and Access will fill in the type closest to your letter. For example, type the letter Y and Access will fill in Yes/No.

1 Open the Plants table you created in Task 3, and move to the first blank row in the **Field Name** column. Type `PropagateBySeed`.

2 Move to the **Data Type** column and select **Yes/No** from the drop-down list.

3 In the **Default Value** text box of the **Field Properties** pane, type `Yes`.

Next Step

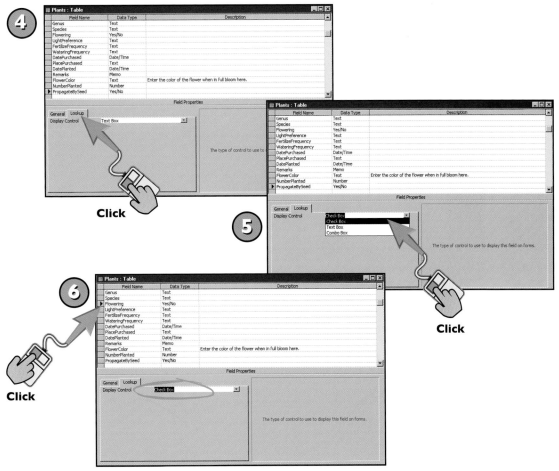

Click

Click

Click

4 Click the **Lookup** tab in the **Field Properties** pane.

5 Select **Check Box** from the option list. A check box appears in both table and form views. Checking the box is the same as saying Yes, removing a check is like saying No.

6 Click the **Flowering** field and change its **Display Control** from **Text Box** to **Check Box** for this Yes/No field.

End Task

Task 7: Saving the New Table Definition

This table definition was already saved once when the Table Wizard finished, but now that you have changed the table structure, you must save it again.

After you save the table structure, Access writes the new definition to your hard disk. This way, all the new fields and properties you've just created will be there the next time you open the table.

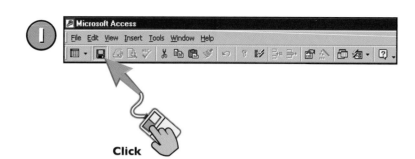

Click

Click

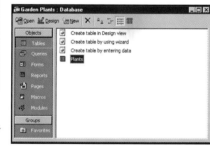

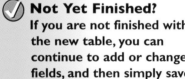

Not Yet Finished?

If you are not finished with the new table, you can continue to add or change fields, and then simply save the revised table definition again.

 Starting where you left off in Task 6, click the Save button on the toolbar. If you did not previously save the table with the wizard, you also must name it.

 When you are finished with the table and have saved it, click the Close (**X**) button at the upper-right corner of the table design window. The new table is now listed in the window.

Task 8: Opening a Table

Start Here!

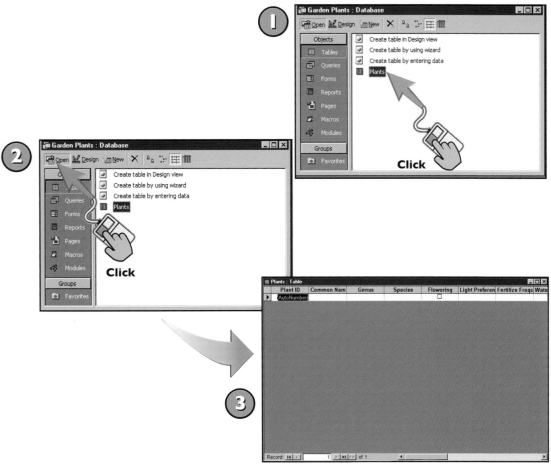

Click

Click

After you have created a table, you must open it in order to work with it, just like you opened the **Access** application to use the databases and table it contains. An unopened table is similar to an unopened ledger or order pad; you can't work with either until you open it.

① Select the **Plants** table by clicking on it.

② Open the table by clicking the **Open** button.

③ The Plants table appears in a datasheet view.

 Opening a Table Shortcut
You can also open the table by using the keyboard shortcut **Alt+O** or by double-clicking the table icon.

End Task

Task 9: Changing a Field Name

As you begin to work with a table, you might find that one or more of the field labels at the top of each column is not as descriptive as you might want it to be. Or even worse, you might find that you accidentally misspelled a label. You can easily change the field label.

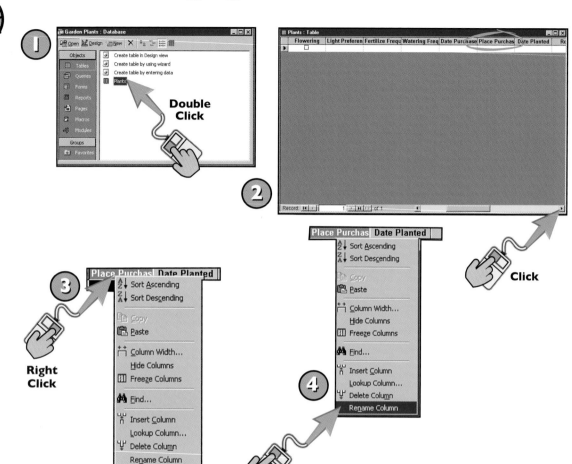

Double Click

Right Click

Click

Click

**Working with Scrollbars**

If you scroll too far, simply click the left scrollbar button to bring the field back in view. It doesn't matter whether the field is in the middle of the window or on one side or the other.

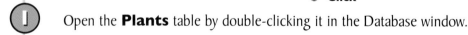

1. Open the **Plants** table by double-clicking it in the Database window.

2. Click the right scrollbar button at the bottom of the table window until you see the field column **PlacePurchased** displayed.

3. Move the mouse pointer to the column label and click the right mouse button to display the shortcut menu.

4. Click on **Rename Column** from the menu. This puts the field label in edit mode. See the blinking cursor at the beginning of the field name.

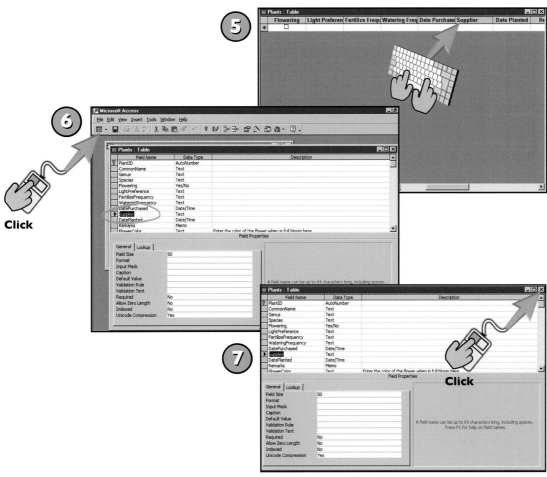

5   Type **Supplier** as the new field label.

6   Click the View button on the toolbar to see the label has been changed there as well.

7   Close the table by clicking the **X** in the corner. Your changes are automatically saved.

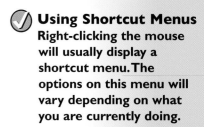

Using Shortcut Menus
Right-clicking the mouse will usually display a shortcut menu. The options on this menu will vary depending on what you are currently doing.

End Task

Task 10: Moving a Field Within a Table

Sometimes after you have worked with a table for a short time you will find the fields are not in the right order. For example, you might input data from a handwritten form that includes a client's Social Security number, last name, and first name. Your table shows the fields in first name, last name, and then Social Security number order.

This discrepancy between the written form and the table requires some fancy eyeball gymnastics that can get very tiring by the end of the day. Simply adjusting the order of the fields in a table takes just a few steps.

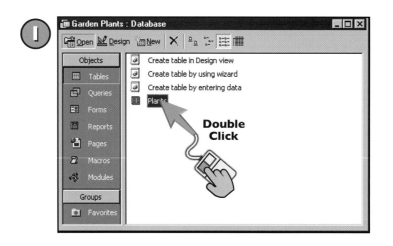

Double Click

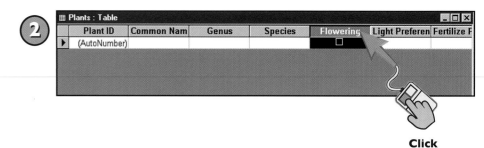

Click

✓ **Table Column Order**
You can change the order of the columns in a table at any time. This does not affect any data in the table, column, or any other object that uses the column.

1 Open the Plants table. You can either select the table and click the **Open** button or double-click the table.

2 Select the column header **Flowering** by clicking it once. Access highlights the entire column.

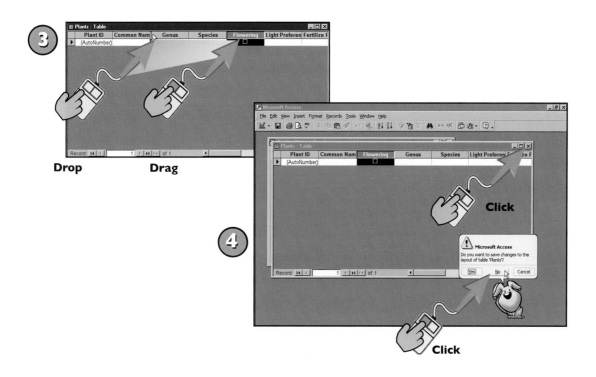

Drop   **Drag**

Click

Click

3 Drag the field to the left of the **Genus** field. As you drag the column, a heavy vertical bar indicates where the column will be placed when you let go of the mouse button.

4 Clicking the Save button can save the new table definition, but don't save this change. Click the Close (**X**) button and then **No** when prompted to save the table.

Task 11: Inserting a Field

As your business or needs change, you might find that not all the information you want is being captured in your table. In just a few seconds you can add a new field to an existing table. It is best to make this decision as soon as possible, otherwise you will have to spend a great deal of time adding this new information to the existing records.

Start Here

Click

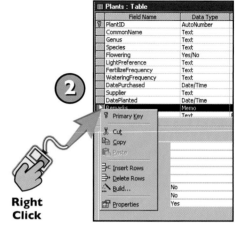

Right Click

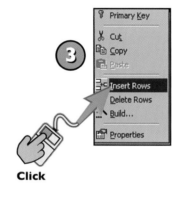

Click

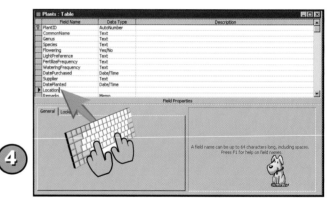

 Where to Insert the Row
When you insert a new row, select the row that will be placed immediately below the newly inserted row.

 Insert Several Rows
You can insert multiple rows by dragging down across as many selector buttons as you want new rows. The number of rows you select is the number of new rows that will be inserted.

 Select the **Plants** table in the Database window and click the **Design** button.

 Place the mouse pointer on the selector button for the **Remarks** field, and right-click to display the shortcut menu.

3 Choose the **Insert Rows** option, and Access will insert a blank line above the **Remarks** row. All other rows are moved down one place.

4 Type **Location** in the **Field Name** column of the new row.

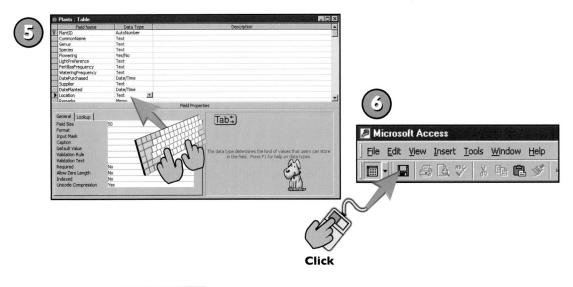

Click

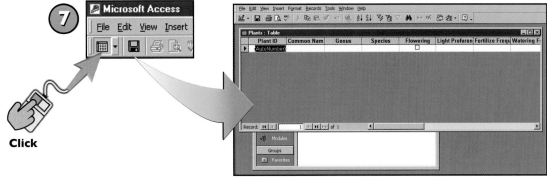

Click

5 Press the Tab key. The default data type **Text** is selected.

6 Click the Save button to save the new table definition.

7 Click the View button to return to the Datasheet view.

✅ **If You Don't Want to Save**
If you decide that you do not want to save the new field, simply select **No** when prompted to save the table.

2

Task 12: Adding a New Field in Datasheet View

Start Here

You can create a new field on the fly while working within the table. You don't have to stop and switch to Design view mode, add the new field, save the table, and then return to the Datasheet view. You can quickly insert a new field into the table and begin adding information to it. The primary disadvantage is that you can't choose a data type or other properties for the field. The new field is inserted as a text field.

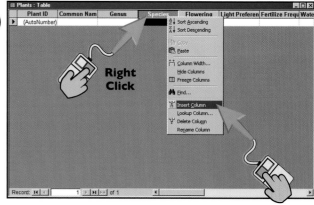

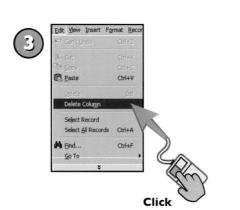

Click

✓ Renaming Columns
You learned to rename a column by selecting it and choosing the **Rename Column** option from the shortcut menu (see Task 9, Step 4).

 Open the Plants table if it is not already open, and select the **Species** field label by clicking it.

 Right-click on the column label, and select **Insert Column** from the shortcut menu. Access inserts a generic field named Field1.

 We don't want to keep the column **Field1**, so select **Edit** from the menu and then **Delete Column**.

Task 13: Deleting a Field

Start Here

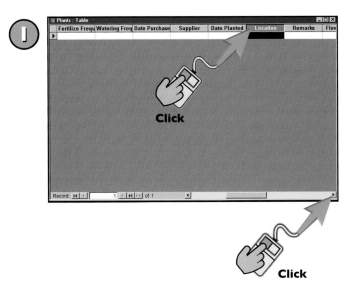

Click

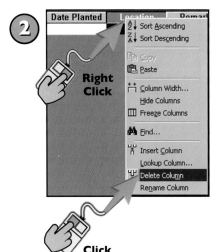
Right Click

Click

Click

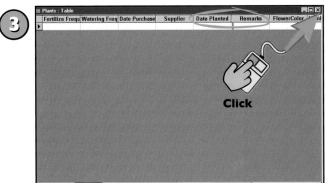
Click

As you begin to use a table in your everyday routine, you might find that you never seem to use one particular field. If you find that a field is not being filled in, is never referred to in a report, or the information is also captured in another table, you can delete the field.

When you delete a field, all the information contained in it is also permanently deleted. You can't recover this information. In addition, any form or report that refers to the field must be corrected.

① Open the Plants table and scroll through the table until you find the **Location** field. Select it by clicking the column label.

② Right-click on the label and select **Delete Column** from the menu. Access will delete the column from the table.

③ Click the Close (**X**) button.

 Deleting a Column
Be absolutely certain that you want to delete a column before doing so. You will not be able to recover the data after the column is gone.

Task 14: Building a Table from Scratch

The tables created with the Table Wizard don't always cover every situation. Using one of them might require you to revise the table, or you can create the table from scratch. By completely creating the table in Design view, you have complete control of the table definition.

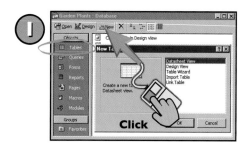

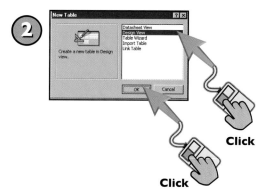

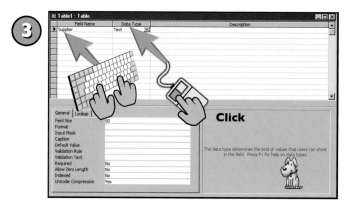

① Be sure the **Tables** option button is selected, and then click the **New** button to display the New Table dialog box.

② Choose the **Design View** option from the list, and then click the **OK** button, opening a blank Design view window.

③ Type **Supplier** as the **Field Name**, and then select **Text** as the **Data Type** for the first row. This will become the primary key field for this table.

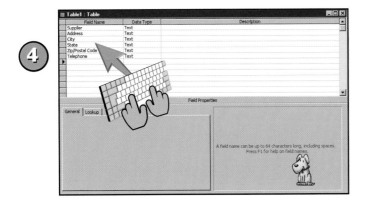

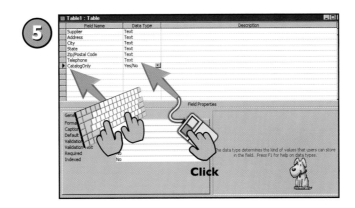

Fixing Misspellings
If you notice a typo in one of your field names, simply select the name and retype it. Editing the field name does not affect any field properties you have set.

Clicking the Wrong Row
If you miss with the mouse and choose the wrong row, just move the mouse and click again. The previously selected row will be deselected and the new row will be selected.

④ Add the following fields in this order: **Address**, **City**, **State**, **Zip/Postal Code**, and **Telephone**. Use the default data type of Text for each.

⑤ In the **Field Name** column of the next row, type **CatalogOnly** and select the **Yes/No** data type.

Building a Table from Scratch Continued

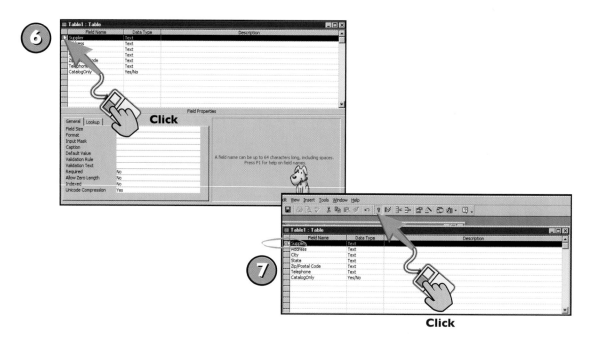

6 Click the selector button for the **Supplier** row. This will highlight the entire row, ensuring you have selected the right row.

7 Click the Primary Key button on the toolbar. Notice the little key symbol now on the selector button.

8 Click the Save button on the toolbar.

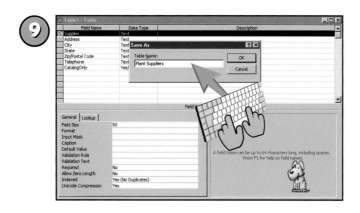

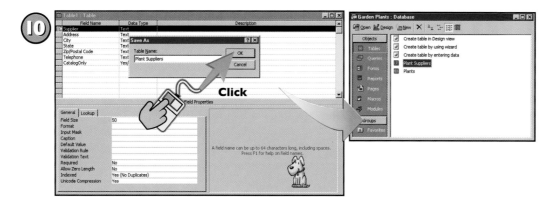

9   Type **Plant Suppliers** as the name for the new table.

10   Click the **OK** button and the new table will be saved. You will see it listed in the Database window after you click the Close (**X**) button.

3

Entering and Editing Data

After you have created the tables for your database, you can begin to enter information into them. Normally, you will enter all the information for each record, and then move on to the next. You can think of each record as a single, blank sheet of paper. After you fill in the necessary information, you can turn to the next blank page and enter the next record.

With a database, you can easily add new information to records and change information with just a few keystrokes. You can even hide selected fields of information from view. This is very helpful if you work with information of a sensitive nature. For example, if you have payroll records, you can easily hide personal information before letting another user view the table.

In addition to being able to easily store large amounts of information, you can quickly find specific records using the powerful Find command. You can also sort records by any field you choose.

In Task I, "Entering New Information Into a Table," you will need to enter the information contained in Tables 3.1 and 3.2 in Appendix A, "Tables." The tables contain the information needed for the records that you will use throughout the rest of this book. Be sure to enter the information exactly as shown, including typos.

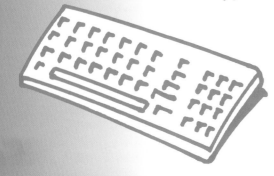

Tasks

Task #		Page #
1	Entering New Information Into a Table	66
2	Completing the Supplier Table	68
3	Copying Information from Another Record	70
4	Editing Data in a Field	72
5	Undoing an Edit	74
6	Searching for Information	76
7	Replacing Selected Information	80
8	Sorting Records	82
9	Using Filters	83
10	Filtering by Form	84
11	Deleting a Selected Record	86
12	Resizing Rows and Columns	88
13	Freezing and Unfreezing Columns	90
14	Hiding and Unhiding Columns	92

Task 1: Entering New Information Into a Table

The reason for creating a database is to store information in a format that you can use. Access stores your information as individual records in the various tables that you create.

When you fill out a paper form, you are completing a record. Each block that you complete is a specific field, whether it is a name, address, date, or quantity.

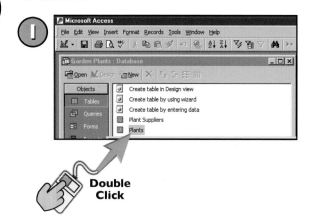

Start Here

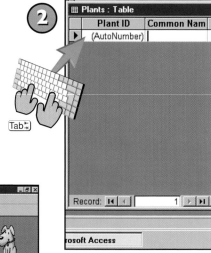

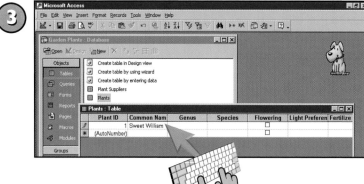

✓ AutoNumbering Fields
The **PlantID** field uses the AutoNumber data type and doesn't allow input. Access always fills in an AutoNumber field.

① Start Access, open the Garden Plants database, and then open the **Plants** table.

② Press the Tab key once, moving the cursor from the **PlantID** field to the **Common Name** field.

③ Type **Sweet William** into the **Common Name** field, and press the Tab key to move to the next field.

Next Step

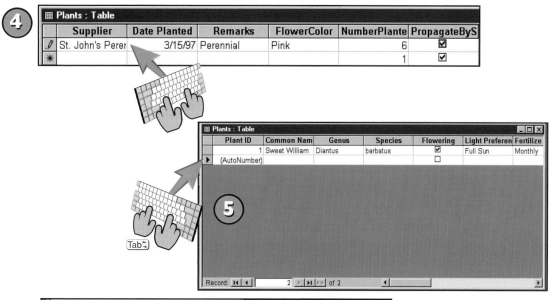

Click

INFO

Using Check Boxes
You also can fill in a check box by pressing the spacebar on your keyboard.

Enter This Information
Genus: Diantus; Species: barbatus; Flowering: check mark; Light Preference: Full Sun; Fertilize Frequency: Monthly; Watering Frequency: Keep Moist; Date Purchased: 3/5/97; Supplier: St. John's Perennials; Date Planted: 3/15/97; Remarks: Perennial; Flower Color: Pink; Number Planted: 6; Propagate By Seed: check mark.

Changing Information
If you make a mistake when entering information into a field, simply press Shift+Tab to move back a field, and then retype.

(4) Finish the record with the information in the "Enter This Information" tip. Press tab between each entry.

(5) Pess the Tab key again. Access automatically saves the new record when you leave the last field.

(6) Complete the table using the information contained in Tables 3.1 and 3.2, repeating steps 2 through 5 for each record. Close the table when you are finished.

Task 2: Completing the Supplier Table

The Plant Suppliers table contains all the information about the suppliers from whom you have purchased plants. Use the techniques learned in Task 1 to enter the necessary information. Table 3.3 in Appendix A, "Tables," contains the information you need.

Start Here

Double Click

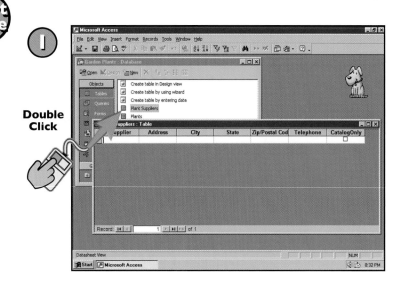

Tab

1 Open the **Plant Suppliers** table by double-clicking its icon in the Database window.

2 Press the Tab key to move from field to field as you enter the information from the table in this task.

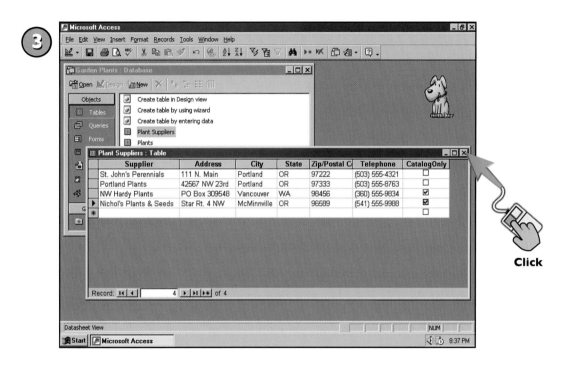

Click

3 Close the table by clicking the Close (**X**) button.

Some information that you enter in your tables for one record will be duplicated in another record, such as the same city or the same state. Even when every record taken as a whole is unique, there might be much repetitive data. Several techniques that you can use when entering or editing information enable you to copy data from one field to another, without having to retype it each time. This can save you much valuable time and help to eliminate errors from miskeying information.

Task 3: Copying Information from Another Record

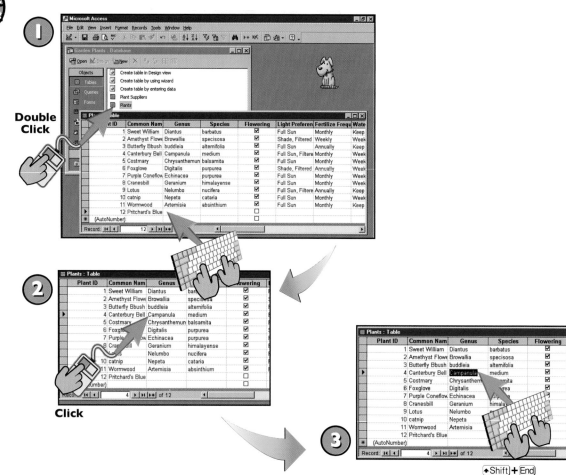

Double Click

Click

(Shift) + (End)

1 Open the **Plants** table, place the mouse pointer in the blank field at the bottom of the **Common Name** column, and click once. Type **Pritchard's Blue** and press Tab.

2 Move the mouse and click in the **Genus** field for the entry **Canterbury Bell**. Press the Home key to move the insertion point to the beginning of the word **Campanula**.

3 Press and hold the Shift key and then press the End key, selecting the entire word, and then let both keys go.

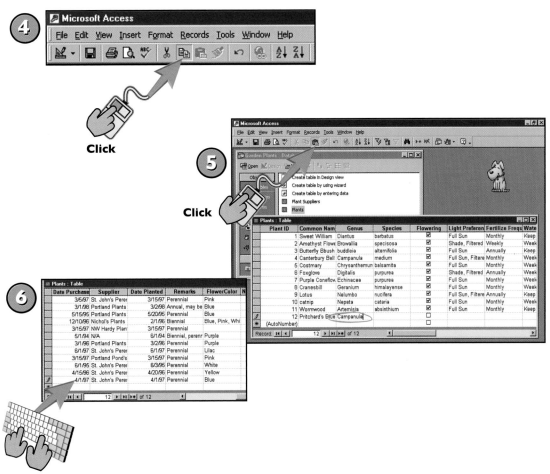

Click

Click

4 Copy the selected text to the Clipboard by clicking the Copy button on the toolbar.

5 Click the mouse inside the empty **Genus** field of the new record, and click the Paste button.

6 Enter the remaining information: **Species**: lactiflora; **Flowering**: check mark; **Light Preference**: Shade; **Fertilize Frequency**: Monthly; **Watering Frequency**: Keep Moist; **Date Purchased**: 4/1/97; **Supplier**: St. John's Perennials; **Date Planted**: 4/1/97; **Remarks**: Perennial; **Flower Color**: Blue; **Number Planted**: 3, and **Propagate By Seed**: check mark.

✓ **Copy Shortcuts**
To copy the contents of the cell directly above another, simply press the keyboard shortcut Ctrl+' (Ctrl key plus the quote mark key).

End Task

Task 4: Editing Data in a Field

In most databases that you will create and use, the information is not static; it changes over time. Companies or people move and change their phone numbers, the number of plants you have increases or decreases, or you might need to correct a name misspelling.

Any of these things will cause you to edit or update a record in a table. Editing information can include correcting an erroneous entry, adding data to a record, deleting a record, or any other change necessary to keep your information accurate.

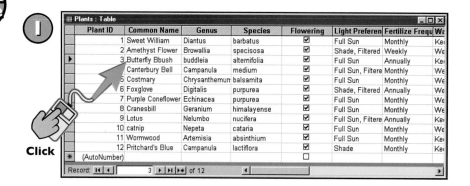

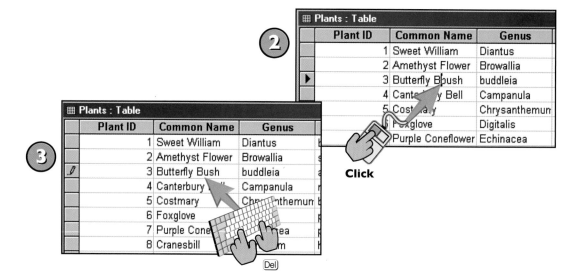

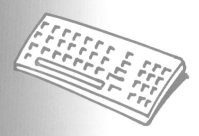

 Click in the field with the entry **Butterfly Bbush**—needless to say, the word "bush" doesn't have two b's in it.

 Place the insertion point between the two b's in **Bbush**.

 Press the Delete key once, deleting the single b to the right of the insertion point.

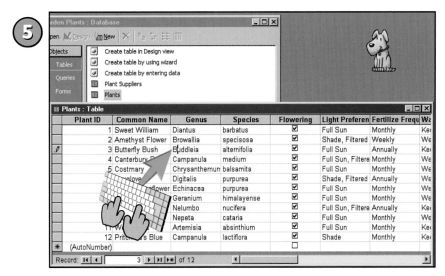

Press the Tab key once, moving to the **Genus** field of the same record and press F2. See the insertion point displayed at the right end of the entry.

Press the Home key to move to the beginning of the entry. Press the Delete key to delete the small b, and type **B** to correct the entry Buddleia.

✅ Deleting to the Left
Use the Backspace key to delete text to the left of the insertion point.

✅ Switching from Navigating to Editing
The F2 key toggles between edit and navigation modes. In navigation mode the arrow keys move you from cell to cell, whereas in edit mode the right and left arrows move you within the cell entry.

✅ Data You Can't Edit
Information can be edited in most cells at any time. You can't edit or enter a value in an AutoNumber field.

Task 5: Undoing an Edit

Start Here

Sometimes as you are making changes to a record, you will find that you accidentally made a change to a field in the wrong record. Access enables you to undo many changes you make to the information in a record as long as you have not yet moved from the field or the record.

After you move from a field, you can undo all the changes to the current record, but not to only a specific field. After you leave the record and begin work in another, you can't undo any previous edits. You must retype the data.

Click

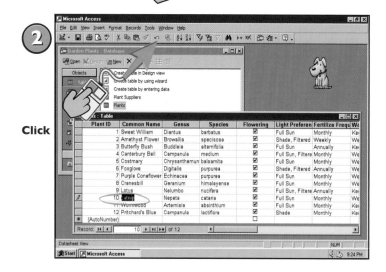

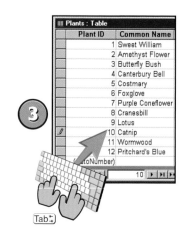

Tab⇥

✓ **Undoing an Edit**
You can undo changes by selecting **Edit, Undo** from the menu. The **Undo** command itself will vary in wording depending on what you are currently doing.

1. Use the arrow keys to move to the **catnip** entry in the **Common Name** column. This selects the entire value. Type **Catnip** to make this entry consistent with the others.

2. Click the Undo button on the toolbar, and you will see that Access has reversed your edit.

3. Type **Catnip** once again and press the Tab key to move to the next field.

Next Step

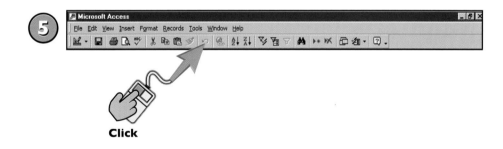

Click

④ Type **Nepetia**, a spelling you believe is correct.

⑤ Press Tab to move to the next field. You recheck a reference and decide that your original spelling was correct, so reverse all the changes you made by clicking the Undo button.

Task 6: Searching for Information

One of the most powerful features of a database is its capability to find information very quickly. How often have you needed to find information about a particular customer or product but not been able to put your hands on the information?

Access normally sorts records by the primary key field, but you can quickly search any field. In a table with many records, using the Find command is much easier than scrolling through the entire table.

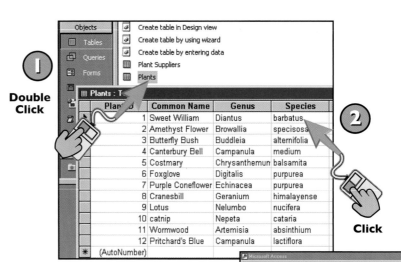

Double Click

Click

Click

1 Open the **Plants** table.

2 Click the mouse pointer in the **Species** field of the first record.

3 Click the Find button on the toolbar. The Find and Replace dialog box appears.

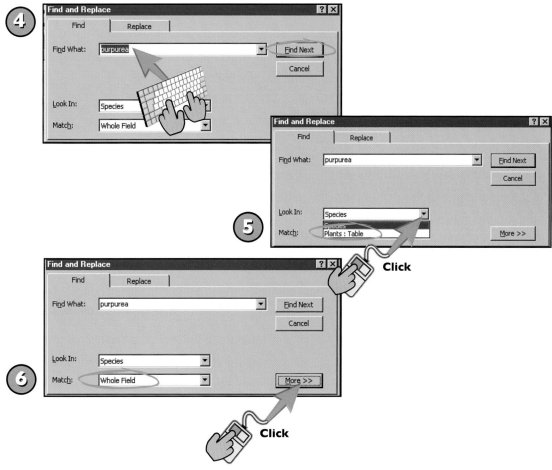

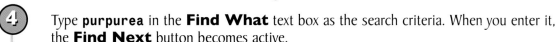

Click

Click

④ Type **purpurea** in the **Find What** text box as the search criteria. When you enter it, the **Find Next** button becomes active.

⑤ If you aren't sure in which field the item you are looking for is located, select **Plants: Table** from the **Look In** combo box.

⑥ In the **Match** combo box, select **Whole Field**. Click the **More** button to see the additional options available to you.

✔️ **Edit Shortcuts**
You can also use the keyboard shortcut Ctrl+F or the **Edit, Find** menu commands to open the Find and Replace dialog box.

✔️ **Searching for Partial Matches**
Access searches for exactly what you enter when the **Whole Field** option is selected. Use **Any Part of Field** to display an item that partially matches, or **Start of Field** to display those matches where the criteria are at the beginning of the field.

Searching for Information Continued

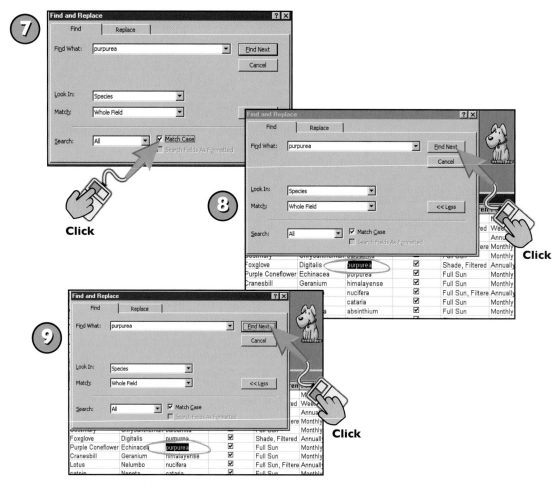

✓ Matching Cases
When **Match Case** is selected, Access finds only purpurea. When deselected, Access finds all matches, including purpurea, Purpurea, and **PURPUREA**.

✓ No Match Found?
If you don't find any matches, try changing some of the search criteria and options in the Find and Replace dialog box.

✓ Move the Find Dialog Box
Drag the Find and Replace dialog box's title bar if it is preventing you from viewing the found record.

 Click the **Match Case** check box to select only those records that exactly match the value you entered in the **Find What** text box.

 Click the **Find Next** button to begin searching. If a match is found, Access moves the record selector indicator to the row and highlights the matching value.

 Click the **Find Next** button again to find any other records meeting your search criteria.

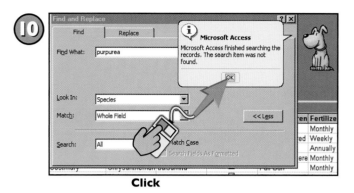

Click

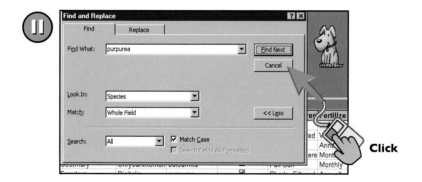

Click

 When no other records are found, the assistant will tell you so. Click **OK** to close this dialog box.

 Click the **Cancel** button to close the Find and Replace dialog box.

Task 7: Replacing Selected Information

The Replace command not only lets you find information, but you can then automatically replace it with a new entry—all in just a few keystrokes and mouse clicks. Replace works very much like Find does, with a few more features. Replace can be especially helpful if you accidentally misspell a city name through a table, or for example, when the phone company changes area codes.

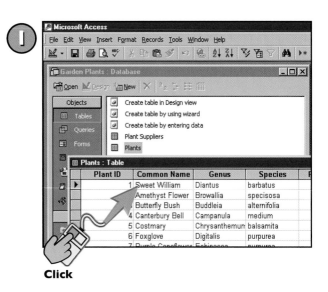

Click

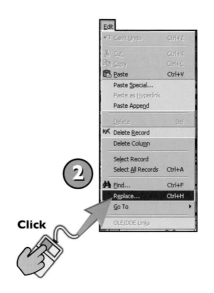

Click

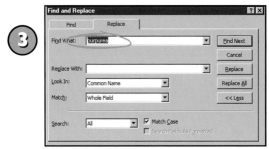

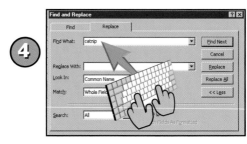

Start Here

✓ **Missing Menu Items**
If an item is not on the menu, pause the mouse on the double-down arrows. After a few seconds, the menu list will expand to include items you have not used or don't use very often.

1 Click the mouse on the first record in the **Common Name** field.

2 Select **Edit**, **Replace** from the menu. Remember, you have not re-edited the entry for catnip.

3 The search criteria you used in the Find tab in Task 6 is shown in the **Find What** text box. Access assumes that the last item you looked for is what you want to replace.

4 Click in the **Find What** text box and type `catnip`, overwriting the previous entry.

Next Step

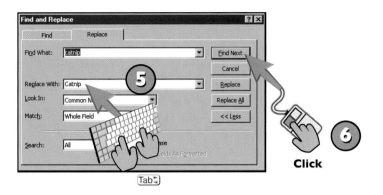

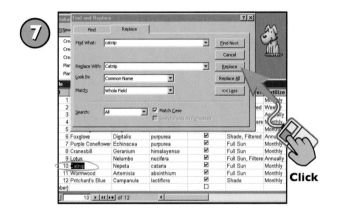

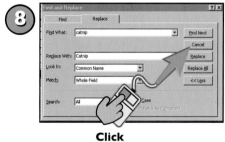

Click

Click

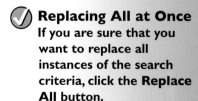

Click

(5) Press the Tab key to move to the **Replace With** text box, and type **Catnip** as the replacement entry.

(6) Click the **Find Next** button, and Access begins searching for the text you have entered. When found, Access highlights the field.

(7) Because this is what you want to replace, click the **Replace** button and the field value will be replaced.

(8) Click the **Cancel** button to close the dialog box.

✓ **Replacing All at Once**
If you are sure that you want to replace all instances of the search criteria, click the **Replace All** button.

Task 8: Sorting Records

From Access, you can easily choose to sort the records in a table by any field you want. Often a table is sorted by a primary key field, which does not make searching for a group of records very easy.
For example, you might want to temporarily sort a customer table by the State field, or you can sort the Plants table by the Common Name field. This is a much simpler way to scroll through your list of plants than in the normal order by PlantID.

Start Here

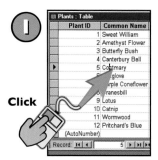

Click

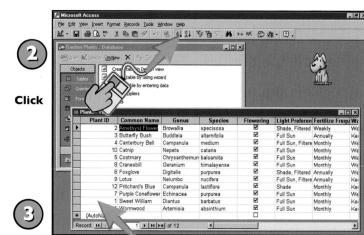

Click

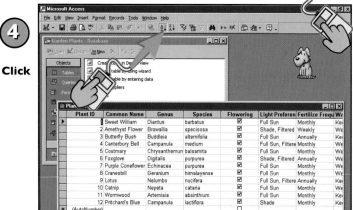

Click

Click

✓ **Sort Orders**
An ascending sort order looks like this: –1, 0, 1, 2, A, B, C, D, ..., Z. Descending is in the opposite direction. Access is not case sensitive.

① Click the mouse anywhere in the **Common Name** column. It does not matter on which record.

② Click the Sort Ascending button on the toolbar. You will now see the table resorted in ascending order by this field.

③ Click in the **Plant ID** column.

④ Click the Sort Ascending button again. You will now see the table in its original order.

End Task

Task 9: Using Filters

Start Here

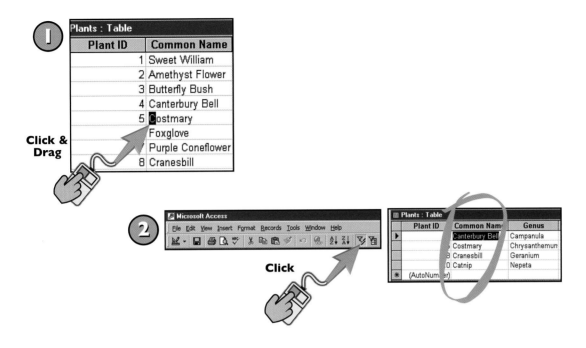

Click & Drag

Click

Click

A filter is a special tool that you can use to display a subset of records from the table. You specify the criteria Access will use to select the records. Use a filter when you want to view or work with only a few records that have something in common. For example, you can filter the Plants table to display only those plants that have blue flowers. In this task, you will filter for all plants whose common name begins with the letter C.

① Place the mouse pointer on the left of the C in **Costmary** and drag across the C to select it.

② Click the Filter By Selection button. You will now see only those plants that have common names beginning with the letter C.

③ Click the Remove Filter button to remove the filter and display all the records in the table.

 Selecting with the Keyboard
If your mouse is giving you a hard time selecting a single letter, you can also select the letter by clicking to the left of it. Then press and hold the Shift key and press the right-arrow key once. This will select the letter.

End Task

Task 10: Filtering by Form

There is another method of filtering information, and that is by form. This is a more powerful method of filtering data, giving you much greater control over which records are displayed. When filtering by form, you can use LIKE and AND operators to select a range of similar records. These types of criteria are covered in greater detail later in Part 5, "Getting Information from the Database." For example, with filter by form, you can view all plants whose common name begins with C and that require full sun.

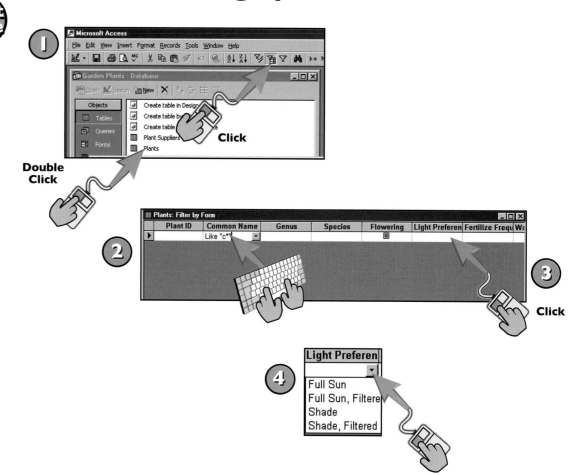

Double
Click

Click

Click

Click

① Open the **Plants** table by double-clicking it, and click the Filter by Form button.

② Click in the **Common Name** field and type **Like "c*"** as the first criterion. Access will filter for all records whose common name begins with c.

③ Click in the **Light Preference** field.

④ Click the arrow button to display the drop-down menu.

Next
Step

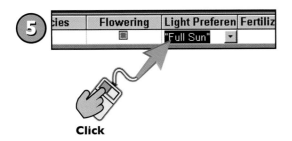

Click

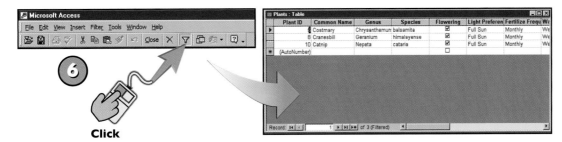

Click

Click

5. Select **Full Sun** from the list as the second criterion a record must meet before it will be filtered into our result set.

6. Display the result set for the filter by clicking the Apply Filter button.

7. Display all the table records by clicking the Remove Filter button.

✓ **What Happened to the Filter Button?**
Notice that the Apply Filter button will move down the toolbar after you apply the filter, and that its name will change to Remove Filter. Same button, different function.

✓ **Saving a Filter**
When you next close the Plants table, you'll be prompted by the assistant to save the changes you have made to the table. The changes include the addition of a filter. If you say Yes, the filter will be saved with the table so that you can use it again.

End Task

Task 11: Deleting a Selected Record

One of the many normal maintenance functions of working with a database is that old, obsolete information must be weeded out or the table begins to take up disk space it doesn't really need. As records are added, you might find others that are unnecessary. For example, you might have records for a customer who no longer buys from you, or a discontinued inventory item, or in the case of the Plants table, an item you no longer grow.

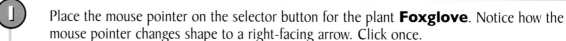

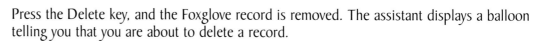

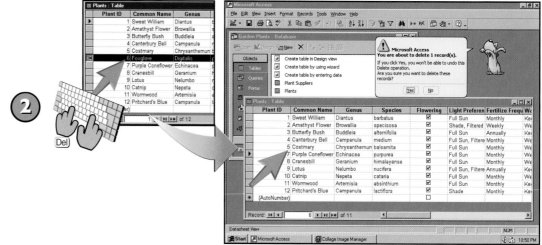

1. Place the mouse pointer on the selector button for the plant **Foxglove**. Notice how the mouse pointer changes shape to a right-facing arrow. Click once.

2. Press the Delete key, and the Foxglove record is removed. The assistant displays a balloon telling you that you are about to delete a record.

Page 86

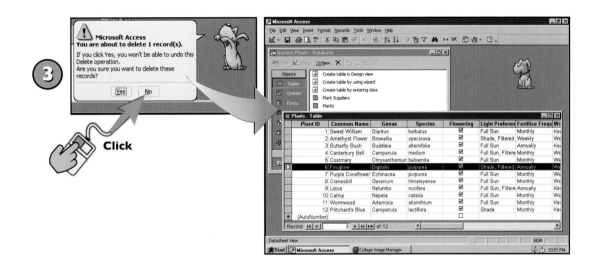

Click

 Click **No**, and the record is returned to its place. If you click the **Yes** option, the record is permanently deleted.

 Other Ways to Delete a Record
You can also use the **Edit, Cut** command on the menu, the Cut button on the toolbar, or the **Delete Record** option on the shortcut menu.

 End Task

Task 12: Resizing Rows and Columns

When Access creates a table, the row width and height are all the same. The height is usually fine for the standard font, but the width might not be wide enough to display all the text. If the information contained in a field is too wide to be shown, only the data that will fit within the column is displayed.

You can easily expand or contract the width of a column or increase and decrease the row height. Changing the row height enables you to display the text of a field in two lines, add more whitespace between records, or show them in a larger font.

Click & Drag

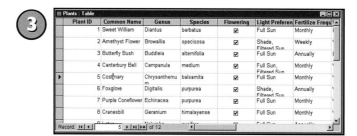

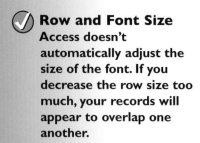

✓ Row and Font Size
Access doesn't automatically adjust the size of the font. If you decrease the row size too much, your records will appear to overlap one another.

1 Change the height of your rows by placing the mouse pointer between any two row selector buttons. See how the pointer changes shape.

2 Drag down to increase the row height. See the dark line extending from the mouse pointer across the table, indicating the size of the row.

3 Release the mouse button and see how all the rows in the table are now the new size.

Next Step

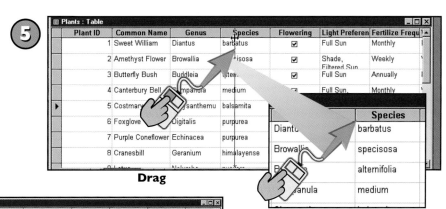

Drag

Drop

Chrysanthemum has dropped its last "m" into a second line. Move the mouse pointer to the dividing point between the **Genus** and **Species** columns. The pointer changes shape.

Drag the column to the right to increase the column width. Again, notice the solid line extending from the pointer.

When you release the mouse button, the column width is reset. Column width changes affect only individual columns. Close and do not save the revised table layout when prompted.

Task 13: Freezing and Unfreezing Columns

When you view or edit information in a table that stretches across many fields and several screen widths, the first few fields that identify each record usually scroll off the screen very quickly. When editing a certain record, it could be very easy to lose track of where you are in the table and accidentally edit the wrong record.

Access enables you to freeze selected columns so that they remain at the farthest-left position in the table at all times. This way the reference columns are always visible.

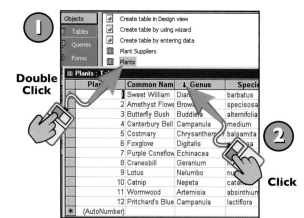

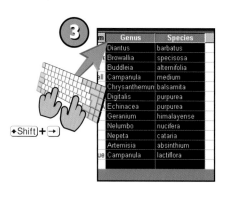

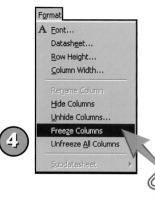

Double Click

Click

Click

⊕Shift+→

✓ **Selecting Several Columns**

You can also choose multiple adjacent columns by dragging across them.

 Open the **Plants** table by double-clicking it.

 Place the mouse pointer on the **Genus** column selector, and when the pointer changes shape to a down arrow, click to select the entire column.

3 Press the keyboard combination Shift+right-arrow to select the **Species** column also.

4 Select **Format** from the menu, and then select **Freeze Columns** from the drop-down menu.

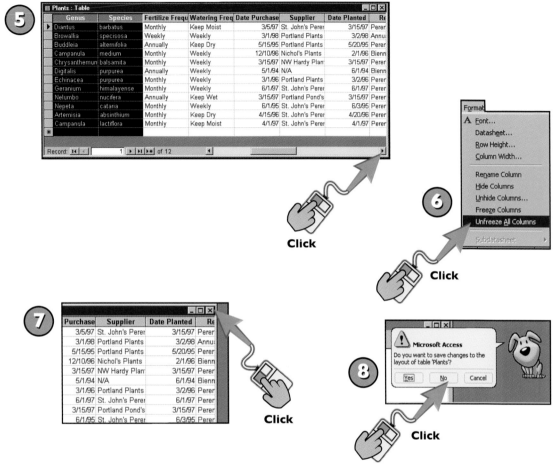

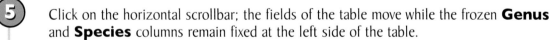

Click

Click

Click

Click

⑤ Click on the horizontal scrollbar; the fields of the table move while the frozen **Genus** and **Species** columns remain fixed at the left side of the table.

⑥ Select **Format**, **Unfreeze All Columns** to unfreeze the columns, remove the dividing bar, and restore normal scrolling. This won't return any columns to their original places.

⑦ Click the Close (**X**) button.

⑧ Choose **No** when prompted to save the new table format. The next time you open the table it will be displayed in its original format.

✓ **Freezing from the Shortcut Menu**
If you are freezing a single column, you can **right-click** on the selected column and choose **Freeze Columns** from the shortcut menu.

✓ **Choosing Columns to Freeze**
You don't have to select the current leftmost column as one of those to freeze in place. You can choose any fields, but they must be adjacent to each other.

Task 14: Hiding and Unhiding Columns

Many people work every day with sensitive, work-related information. When using such tables, you might want to hide from view those columns containing the sensitive data. For example, you might be helping a coworker gather statistical information about employee salaries, but you don't need to show them how much money a particular individual is paid. You can easily hide identifying information such as employee ID and name.

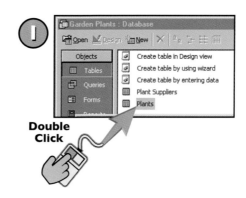

Double Click

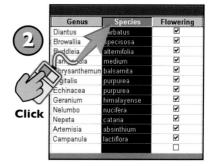

Click

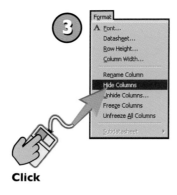

Click

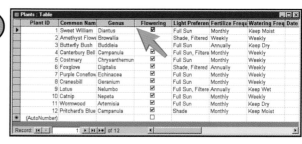

① Open the **Plants** table by double-clicking it.

② Move the cursor to the column you want to hide—such as the **Species** column—and select it by clicking on the column selector button.

③ Click **Format**, **Hide Columns**.

④ Access immediately hides the selected columns from view.

Click

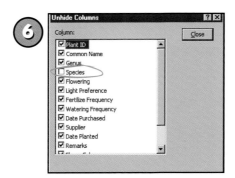

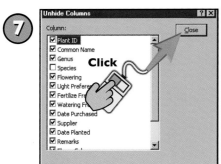

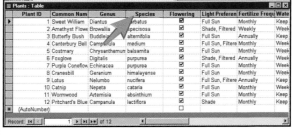

(5) Unhide the columns by selecting **Format**, **Unhide Columns**. This will display the Unhide Columns dialog box.

(6) The **Species** column, which is currently hidden, doesn't have a check mark beside it. Click inside the box. The table blinks behind the dialog box as Access unhides the **Species** column.

(7) Click the **Close** button to return to the table and see how the **Species** column is now displayed in its normal place.

✓ **Hiding Multiple Columns**
You can hide any number of adjacent columns by dragging across all of them, and then selecting **Format, Hide Columns** from the menu.

✓ **Using Unhide Columns to Hide Columns**
You can use the Unhide Columns dialog box to hide columns that aren't adjacent to each other by selecting **Format, Unhide Columns** from the menu, and then removing the check marks for all columns you want to hide.

End Task

Using Database Forms

Implementing forms is a more user-friendly way to view and input information into a database. Most of the forms that you will use are based on either a table or a query. They can be used to edit existing records, display calculated values, display information from multiple tables, or create a custom switchboard or dialog box.

Commonly, you will create forms that mimic a paper form that you currently are using. For example, you can easily create a sales order form that will allow you to enter an order directly into the computer. The form will also automatically fill in current prices and calculate totals.

Tasks

Task #		Page #
1	Using an AutoForm	96
2	Using a Wizard to Build a Form	98
3	Opening the Form Design View Window	102
4	Adding Fields to a Form	104
5	Moving Fields in Form Design	106
6	Creating Headers and Footers	108
7	Creating Labels	110
8	Using a Combo Box	112
9	Adding a List Box	116
10	Moving Objects	118
11	Editing a Label	120
12	Using an Option Button	122
13	Adding a Calculated Field	124
14	Adding Pop-Up Tip Text to Fields	128
15	Using Color in the Form	130
16	Saving Your New Form	132
17	Opening a Form	133
18	Entering and Editing Information with a Form	134
19	Changing the Field Order	136

Task 1: Using an AutoForm

Start Here

You can quickly create a form from the currently selected or open object such as a table or query. With just the click of a button, Access will build a simple form based on this object. You can use the **New Object** button on the toolbar to create an **AutoForm**. Whenever you want to easily view records from a table without creating a new form, simply click the **New Object** button.

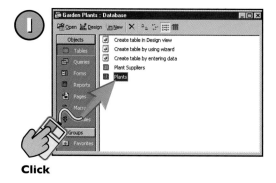

Click

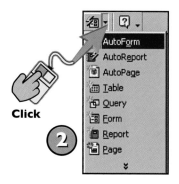

Click

②

✅ **The New Object Button**
If you opened the Plants table, continue to step 2. The New Object button works just as well on an open table.

③

Click

✅ **Not Yet Installed?**
If the Office Assistant prompts you that the AutoForm or other object is not installed, insert the program CD-ROM and click **OK**. The object is installed for you.

① Open the Garden Plants database, and then select the **Plants** table by clicking it once.

② Click the down arrow on the right side of the New Object button to display the drop-down menu of options.

③ Select the **AutoForm** option.

Next Step

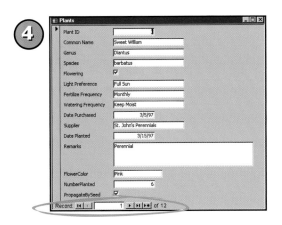

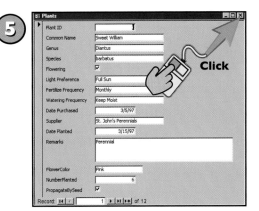

Click

Click

4 After the AutoForm is displayed, you can use the Page Down key or the record navigation buttons at the bottom of the form to view more records.

5 Click the Close (**X**) button.

6 Click the **No** button when prompted to save the form.

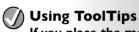

Using ToolTips
If you place the mouse pointer on the New Object button, the ToolTip **New Object: AutoForm** is displayed. Click the left side of the button to display the AutoForm.

Task 2: Using a Wizard to Build a Form

When you are ready to design a form with more features and controls than a simple AutoForm, try using the Form Wizard. It helps you design a form with special backgrounds, colors, and customized fields and label styles.

The wizard guides you through a series of dialog boxes, each focusing on a different aspect of the form's design. When the wizard is finished, a complete form will be displayed based on your selections.

✓ **Saved Forms Appear on the Database Window**

Any new form that you create and save will be listed in this Database window, just as the tables you have created are shown in the Tables window.

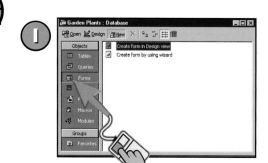

Start Here

Click

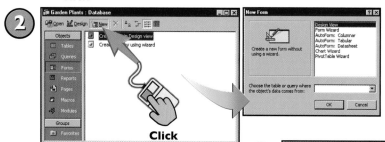

Click

Click

Click the **Forms** object button on the Database window.

Click the **New** button, or press Alt+N.

From the New Form dialog box, select the **Form Wizard** option.

Next Step

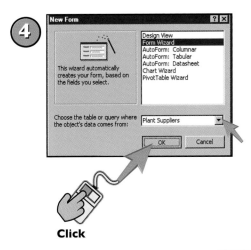

Click

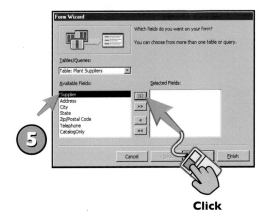

Click

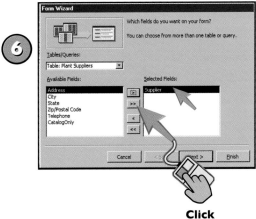

Click

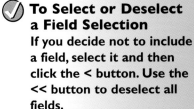

Using the combo box below, select **Plant Suppliers**, and then click **OK**.

Use the **Available Fields** list to select the fields to be included on your form. Select the **Supplier** field, then click the **>** button, moving the field to the **Selected Fields** box.

Because you want to include all the fields from the Plant Suppliers table, click the **>>** button to include all the fields.

 To Select or Deselect a Field Selection
If you decide not to include a field, select it and then click the **<** button. Use the **<<** button to deselect all fields.

Selecting a Layout
Select one of the four layout options by clicking its option button. The example will change as you click each option.

Using a Wizard to Build a Form
Continued

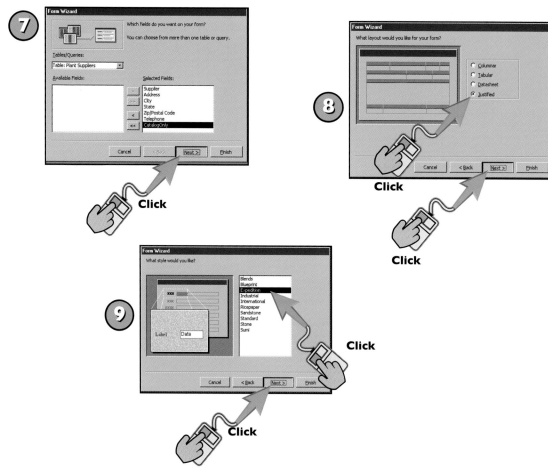

⑦ Click the **Next>** button.

⑧ Click the **Justified** option, and then click the **Next>** button.

⑨ Select a style for the background, fields, and labels. Click the **Expedition** option, then click the **Next>** button.

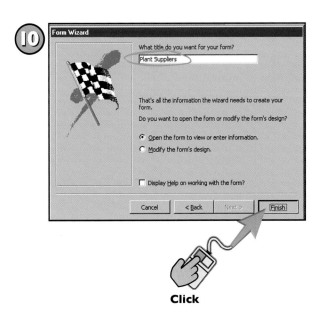

Click

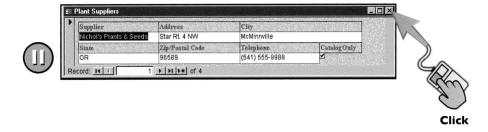

Click

 You can now enter a title for your form. The default name is the same as the object the form is based on. Click the **Finish** button, and Access will build the form.

 Enter the new records using the form, and they will be entered into the Plant Suppliers table. Click the Close (**X**) button.

 If You Don't Use a Form
If you find that you don't use the form, you can always delete or revise it to make it more functional.

Task 3: Opening the Form Design View Window

Whenever you want to edit the design of an existing form or create a new form from scratch, you will do so using the Form Design view window. From here you have the greatest control over all aspects of a form's design. You will be able to make all the decisions about the placement and appearance of fields, labels, and other objects.

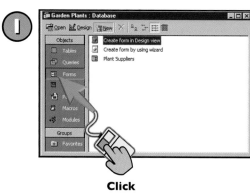

Click

Click

Click

 Click the **Forms** tab on the Database window. You will see the Plant Suppliers form that you just created.

 Click the **New** button.

 On the New Form dialog box, select **Design View** from the list.

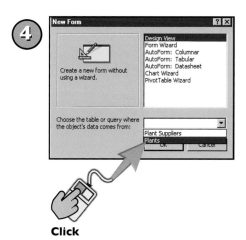

Click

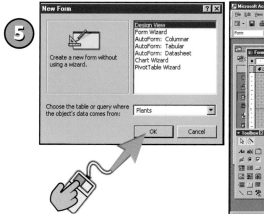

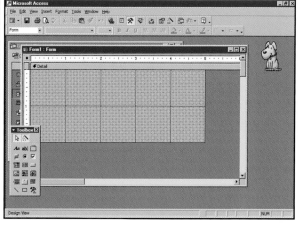

Click

(4) Choose **Plants** from the combo box as the base for the form.

(5) Click **OK**, and the Form Design window is displayed.

✓ **New Toolbars!**
Notice that the Standard toolbar has now been replaced by two new toolbars: Form Design and Formatting. There is also a floating toolbox called Toolbox.

Task 4: Adding Fields to a Form

The primary purpose of creating a form is to simplify the viewing, adding, and editing of information contained in a table. This is done through the fields on the form, which are linked directly to the fields in the table.

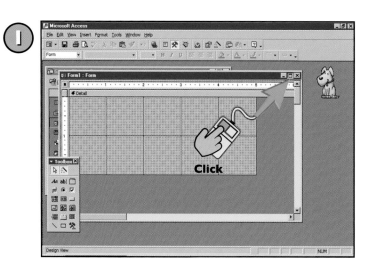

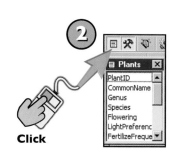

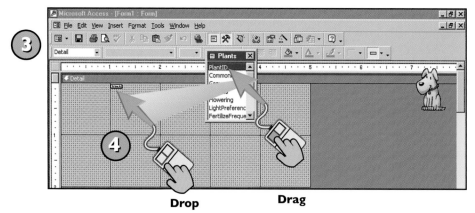

Drop   **Drag**

  Maximize the Form Design window by clicking the Maximize button.

  Click the Field List button on the toolbar. This displays a floating list box with the fields that are available from the object on which the form is based.

  Click and drag the **PlantID** field from the Field List box to the **Detail** area of the form. The mouse pointer changes shape to represent a field.

  Place the field beside the black one-inch grid line, and drop the field by releasing the mouse button.

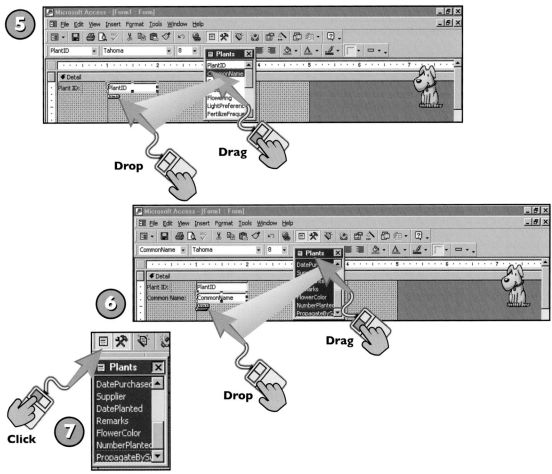

Will the Real Field Stand Up?
When you place a field on the grid, you will actually see that two boxes are added. The right box is the actual field, while the one on the left is the field label.

Using the Rulers
Use the horizontal and vertical rulers to help you estimate the placement of the field.

⑤ Select the **CommonName** field from the list box and drag it to the form **Detail** area beneath the one you just placed.

⑥ To select the remaining fields, click **Genus** and scroll down to the last field. Hold the Shift key while clicking on the last field. Now drag and drop the group onto the form grid.

⑦ Close the Field List box by clicking either the Field List button or the Close (**X**) button on the Field List box.

Task 5: Moving Fields in Form Design

Unless you are extremely adept at placing your fields in the right location every time, you will need to move some of them to different locations. This is especially true when you drag and drop multiple fields. These fields are placed in a simple columnar format, and you can get this same arrangement from the AutoForm.

Fields can be moved anywhere on the form grid. They can be moved with or independently of their labels, and they can be moved as a group. You can also adjust the size of a label or field.

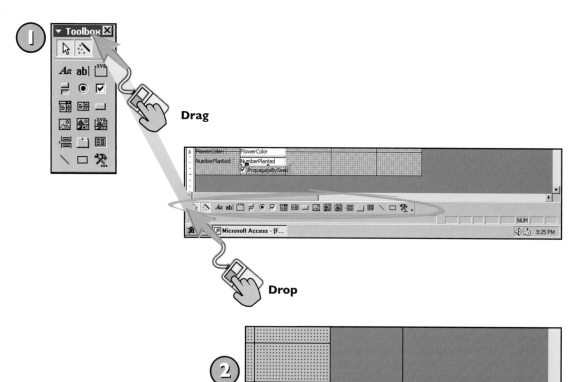

Drag

Drop

Drag

Drop

Click the title of the toolbox and drag it to the bottom of your screen. When the outline changes from vertical to horizontal, release it to dock it at the bottom of the window.

Enlarge the form grid by dragging the bottom-right corner of the grid to the size that you want on the rulers. The mouse changes shape to a four-headed arrow.

Next
Step

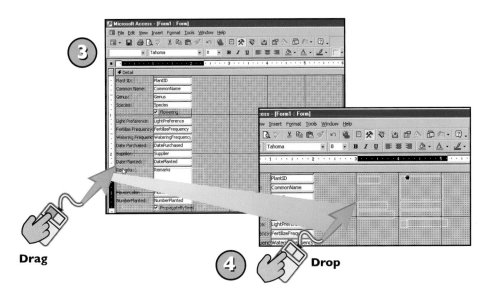

3

Drag

4 **Drop**

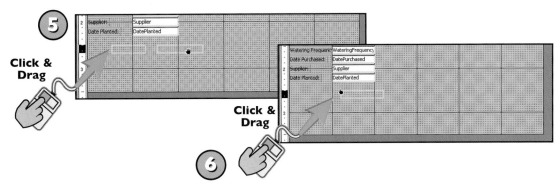

5

Click & Drag

Click & Drag

6

3 Select the last four fields and labels by clicking the form grid near one of the fields and dragging a box around them. You don't have to completely surround a field to include it.

4 Drag the group to the right and top of the Detail area, and drop them.

5 Move a single field by clicking and dragging it. Notice the mouse pointer again changes shape to an open hand.

6 Move just an individual field or label by dragging the large handle in its upper-left corner. The mouse changes to a hand with a pointing finger.

The Check Box Control
Fields that use the Yes/No data type are displayed on a form with a **Check Box** control. You can change the formatting later if you want.

Using Handles
Notice the eight black squares surrounding the field box. These are called handles. You can resize a field or label with these handles.

End Task

Task 6: Creating Headers and Footers

Start
Here

You use headers and
footers to place information
that is repeated only at the
top and bottom of the
form. A header area is often
used to place information
such as a title, a company
logo, the date, and other
information. The form
footer area can be used for
calculated fields, such as the
total of an invoice, or other
summary information that
you often find at the
bottom of a paper form.

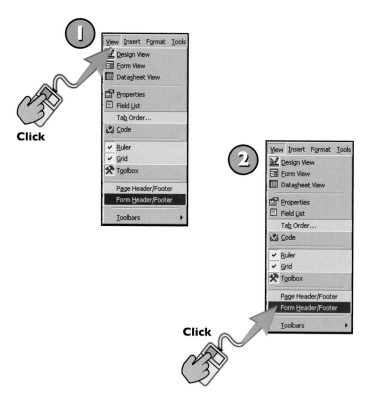

Click

① Select **View** from the menu.

② Click the **Form Header/Footer** option from the menu.

Next
Step

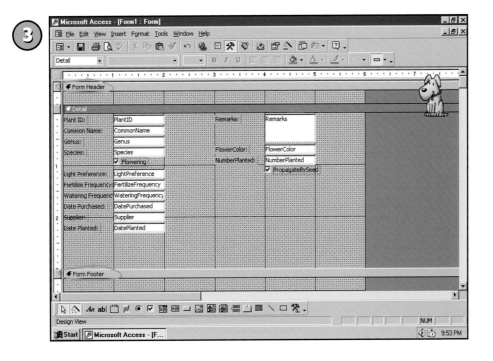

3 You will see two new grid sections added to your form, the header at the top and the footer at the bottom.

Task 7: Creating Labels

You use labels on forms for several reasons: as a title or subtitle, to give definition to different parts of a form, and to give instructions. You might have your own needs for adding labels to a form. They can help you give your form a more professional appearance, and they make your form easier to use.

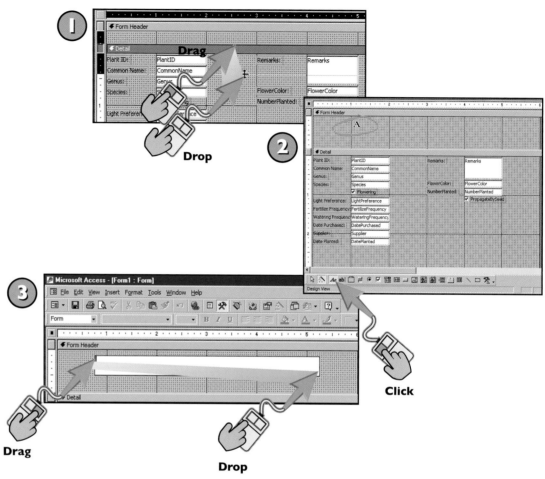

Start Here

(✓) Using the Ruler to Help with Object Placement
When you move an object or change its size, notice how a black band is displayed on both the vertical and horizontal rulers, indicating the current size and placement.

1. Increase the size of the header grid by clicking the top of the **Detail** bar and dragging down. The mouse changes shape to a horizontal bar with arrows.

2. Click the Label button on the toolbox at the bottom of the screen. The mouse changes shape to the letter A with a plus sign.

3. Drag to create a box. A blank label box is displayed with a blinking cursor inside.

Next Step

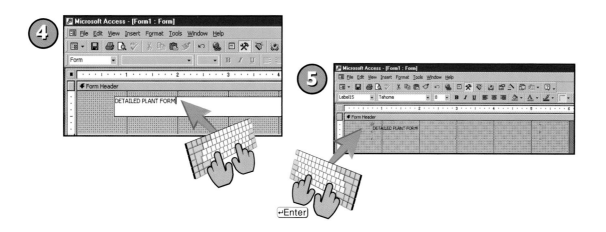

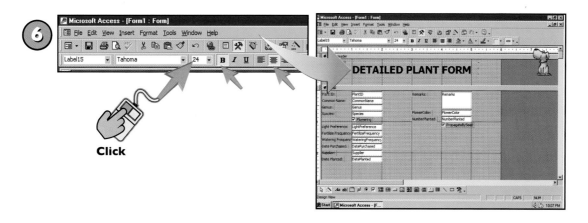

4 Type **DETAILED PLANT FORM** as the title for this form.

5 Press the Enter key to switch out of edit mode, and select the new label.

6 On the toolbar, click the Bold and Center buttons, and then change the font size from **8** to **24**.

Click

✅ **Change a Label's Size with Handles**
If the text doesn't fit inside your label, simply select it and use the handles to increase its size.

✅ **If You Have an Unwanted Label**
If you decide that you don't need a label, simply select it and then press the Delete key.

Task 8: Using a Combo Box

The combo box is a versatile method of getting data into a form. You can restrict the choices a user has to only one of a list of options, or you can allow them to type something else. Combo boxes can help you ensure that your data is consistent for the most frequently used information, but still flexible enough to meet all your needs. Information in a combo box can be based on a list of values you enter when you create the control, or on a query or table. If you must frequently update the choices displayed, base the control on a table or query. Changing this information is easier than changing the control list.

Start Here

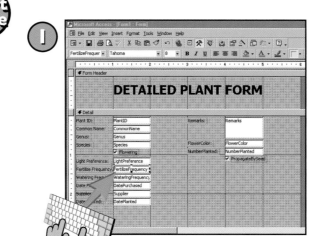

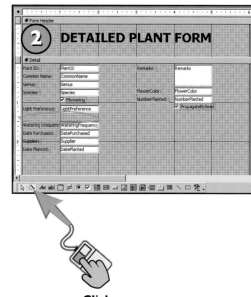

Click

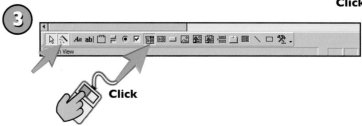

Click

✓ **Deleting a Label Doesn't Delete the Field**
If you accidentally delete only the field label, the field will remain on the form. Simply select the field and delete it.

 Select the **FertilizeFrequency** field on your form and press the Delete key. Remember to select the field, not its attached label.

 The field is removed from your form, but not from the underlying table. Click the Control Wizards button on the toolbox, if not already depressed.

 Click the Combo Box button. Notice that the Control Wizards button remains depressed. It is used in combination with other buttons.

⑤

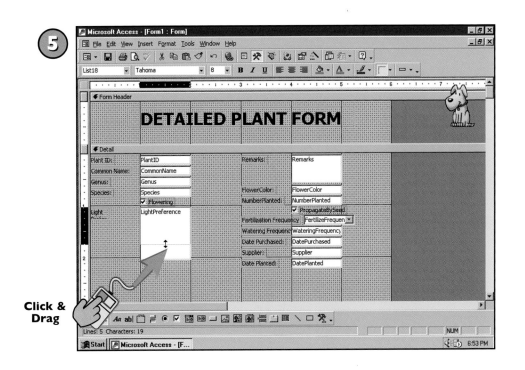

Click & Drag

⑤ Select the **LightPreference** field and drag its bottom resize handle up until it is approximately 3/4-inch high.

✓ **An Alternative Way to Select Objects**
You can also select objects that aren't adjacent to each other by pressing and holding the Shift key while you click each object that you want to move.

✓ **Adjusting Field Positions**
If your fields end up being slightly to one side or the other, just drag them back into place.

End Task

Task 11: Editing a Label

As you continue to design your form, you might find that some of the default labels assigned to your fields don't adequately describe the information that should be entered. In order for your form to be of real use to its user, they should be able to know what information is required for a field simply by reading its label.

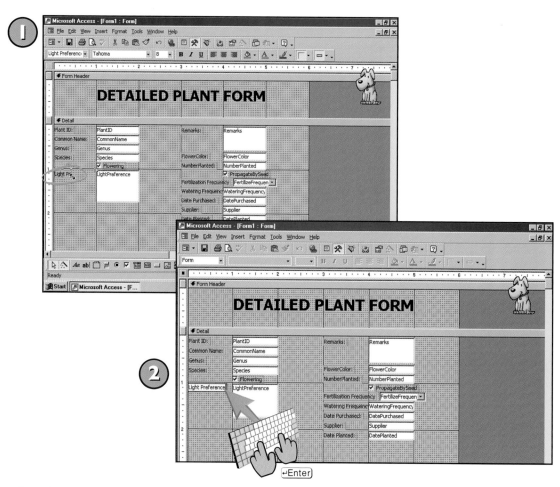

Switching to Edit Mode
You can also press the F2 key to switch into and out of edit mode.

 Select the attached label for the **LightPreference** field, which now reads **Light P**.

 Press Enter to switch to edit mode, placing the insertion point at the end of the label's text.

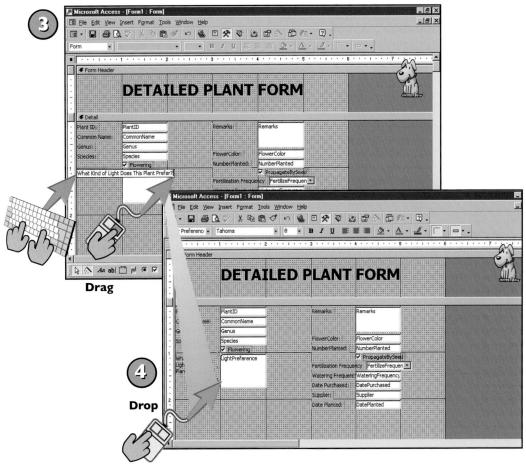

Drag

Drop

(3) Delete the label text using the Backspace key, and type **What Kind of Light Does This Plant Prefer?**. The label stretches across the field. Press Enter to toggle out of edit mode.

(4) Select and drag the lower-right corner of the label. The label can now hold three lines of text.

Task 12: Using an Option Button

Several controls enable you to enter a Yes/No type of response: toggle buttons, option buttons, and check boxes. Option buttons and check boxes can be used in both forms and reports, whereas toggle buttons can be used only on forms. Each of these work in much the same way, so only option buttons are discussed here.

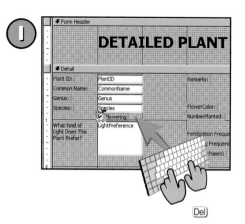

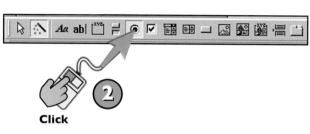

Click

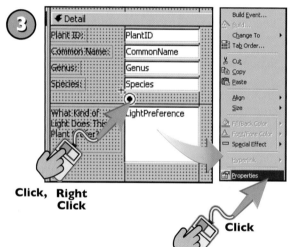

Click, Right
Click

Click

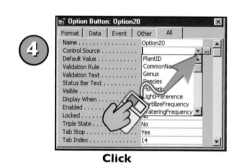

Click

✓ **Open the Property Sheet**

You can also open the property sheet by selecting the object and clicking the Properties button on the toolbar.

 Select the **Flowering** field, and press the Delete key to remove it from the form.

 Click the Option Button tool on the toolbox, and move the mouse to where the **Flowering** field had been located.

 Click once, and an option button control is placed on your form. Right-click the option button and select **Properties** from the shortcut menu. The property sheet opens.

 Press the down-arrow key to select the **Control Source** text box. Click the arrow button on the combo box to display the list of available field objects.

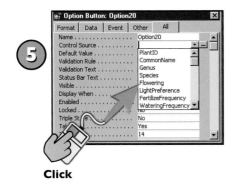

Click

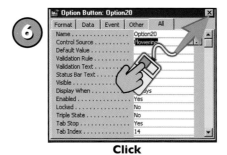

Click

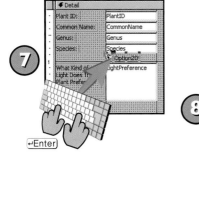

←Enter

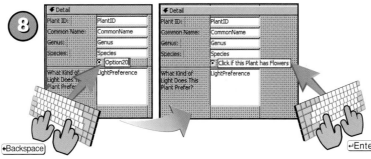

←Backspace

←Enter

(5) Select **Flowering** from the list. This is the field that controls this object button.

(6) Close the property sheet by clicking its Close (**X**) button.

(7) Select the label for the option button, and press Enter to switch to edit mode.

(8) Backspace to delete the existing label and type **Click if this Plant has Flowers**. Press Enter again to switch out of edit mode.

 The Default Flowering Button
When you click this button, Access enters a Yes into this field in the Plants table.

 End Task

Task 13: Adding a Calculated Field

You can use calculated fields for many different things. A calculated field can combine information from two or more fields into a single field. You can use a calculated field to perform arithmetic functions (add, subtract, multiply, and divide) between two fields such as a quantity and a price to give the extended price. You can also use a calculated field to sum a group of numbers and display the total.

In this example, you will create a calculated field that will sum the number of plants you have planted.

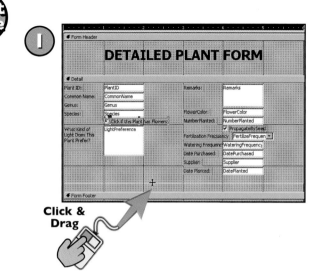

Start Here

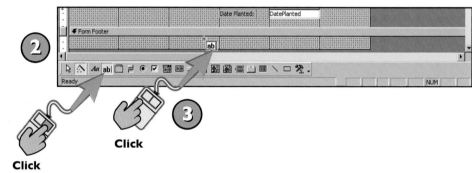

Click & Drag

Click

Click

1. Drag the **Form Footer** bar up so that you can view everything in a single screen.

2. Click the Text Box button on the toolbox and bring it up to the form footer area.

3. Click once, and Access will place an unbound text box on the form footer.

Next Step

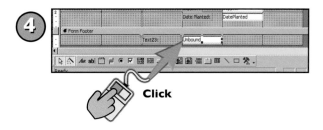

Click

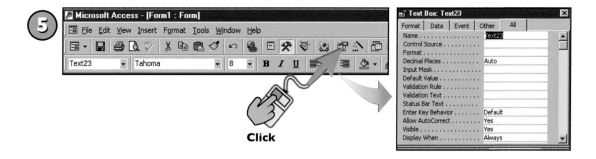

Click

④ Select the text box field—it says **Unbound** inside it.

⑤ Click the Properties button on the toolbar. The property sheet for the text box displays.

Adding a Calculated Field Continued

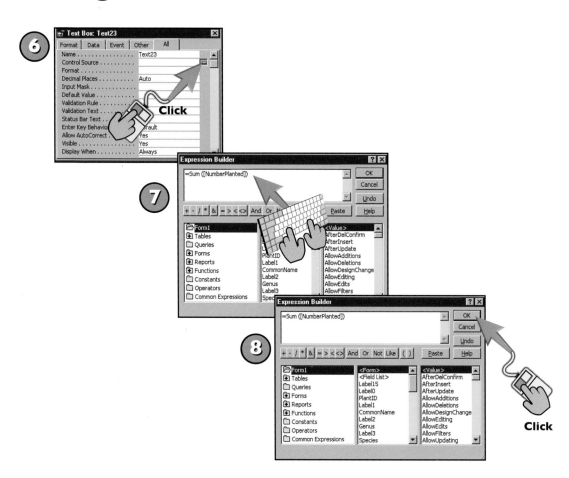

Selecting Fields for a Formula

When using fields in a formula, select them from the middle list box. This ensures that you do not make a mistake in the spelling and have your formula fail.

6 Select the Control Source box, and then click the build (...) button beside it. This will open the Expression Builder dialog box.

7 Type the formula **=Sum ([NumberPlanted])** into the text box. You can also select operators, functions, and fields from the lists below.

8 Click **OK** on the Expression Builder dialog box.

Click

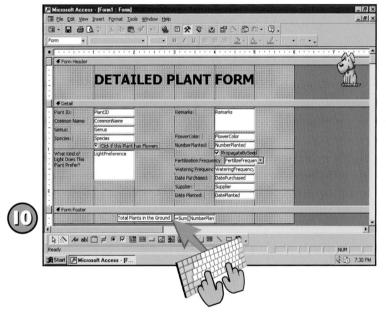

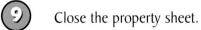

Close the property sheet.

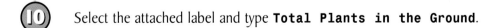

Select the attached label and type **Total Plants in the Ground**.

Task 14: Adding Pop-Up Tip Text to Fields

In addition to the other forms of help you have learned to use, Access enables you to create your own pop-up tips that are displayed when a user pauses the mouse pointer on a field in the form. These tips act just like the ToolTips you have seen when placing the mouse on a tool on the toolbar.

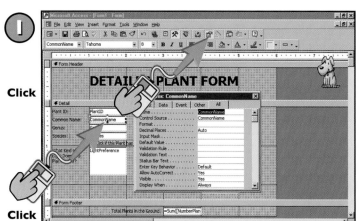

Click

Click

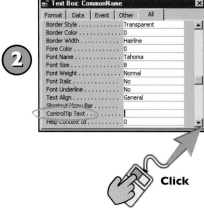

Click

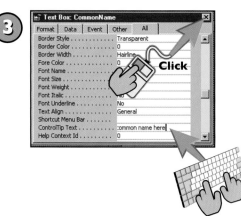

Click

① Select the **CommonName** field, and then click the Properties button on the toolbar.

② On the properties sheet, scroll down the list until you come to the **ControlTip Text** property.

③ Type `Type the Plant's common name here`. Close the Property Sheet by clicking the Close (**X**) button.

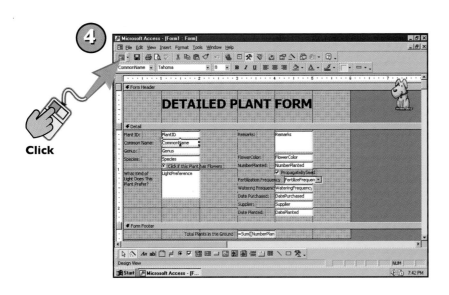

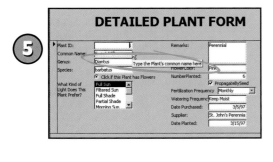

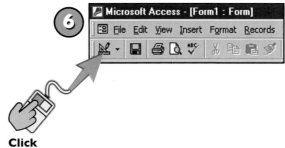

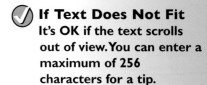

Click

Click

④ Click the View button on the toolbar, and the form will be displayed in Form view.

⑤ Place the mouse pointer on the **CommonName** field and see the tip displayed. This is a good method of seeing how your form currently looks.

⑥ Click the View button again to return to form design view.

✅ **If Text Does Not Fit**
It's OK if the text scrolls out of view. You can enter a maximum of 256 characters for a tip.

Task 15: Using Color in the Form

When you create a form, Access uses the default Windows colors, which are a nice mid-range gray. Changing them is easy. You can use colors for the background, fields, labels, and the text within them, and can apply different colors to text labels and field labels. You can do many things with color to make your form more interesting and easier to use.

Overusing color can be very easy. Be consistent in your use, and don't make fields or text hard to see because of the colors you select.

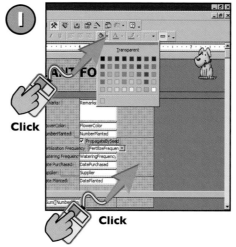

Click

Click

Click

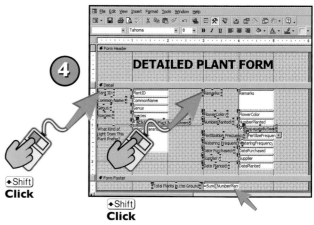

Click

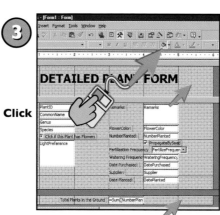

Click

◆Shift)
Click

◆Shift)
Click

(1) Click anywhere on the background of the form **Detail** area, and click the down-arrow button next to the Fill/Back Color button.

(2) Because this is a plant form, select the pale green color for the form's background by clicking the color on the palette.

(3) Click on both the Form Header and Footer and click the Fill/Back Color button. The last selected color will be used for the background.

(4) Select all the field labels in both the Detail area and the Footer. Remember to hold down the Shift key while you click each label to select them all.

Next Step

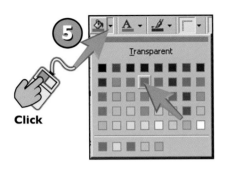

Transparent

Click

Click

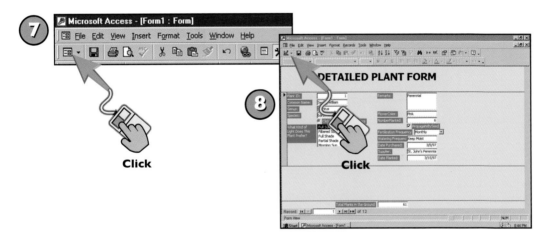

Click

Click

5. Click the down-arrow button of the Fill/Back Color button to display the palette again. Select a dark green color for the labels.

6. A dark background and black text are usually difficult to read. Click the down-arrow button on the Font/Fore Color button, and select the white color button.

7. Click the View button to see how the form now looks.

8. Click the View button once again to return to the Form Design window.

Task 16: Saving Your New Form

After you have completed your form, you must save it or you will lose all your work. Access doesn't automatically save a form created in Design view like it did the form created with the wizard. When you save the form, it is placed on the Forms list and is available for later use.

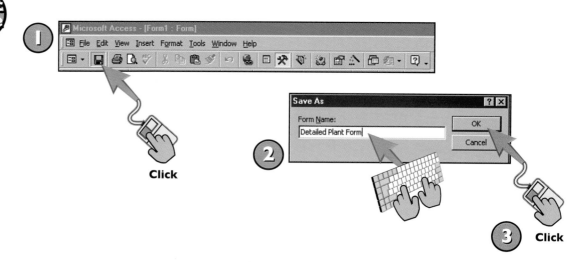

Start Here

Click

Click

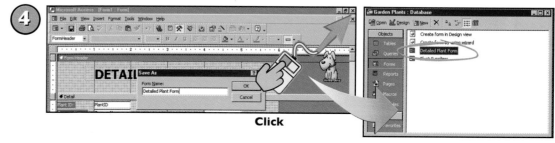

Click

✓ **Save Shortcuts**
You can also select **File, Save** from the menu or press the **Ctrl+S** keyboard shortcut to do the same thing.

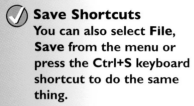

1 Click the Save button on the toolbar, and the Save As dialog box appears.

2 Type **Detailed Plant Form** into the **Form Name** text box. This is the name that will be displayed on the Forms list in the Database window.

3 Click the **OK** button.

4 Click the Close (**X**) button on the form window. You will now see your form in the Forms list.

End Task

Task 17: Opening a Form

Click

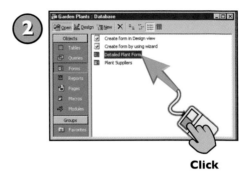

Click

Just like a table on which a form is based, you must open the form before you can do any work with it. After you open the form, you can enter or edit information in the table. Remember that the form is simply another way to view the information contained in the table.

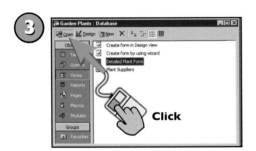

Click

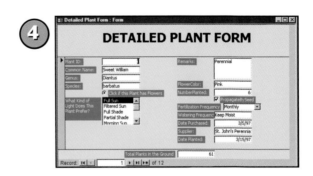

(1) Click the Forms object button on the Database window to display the list of forms now available.

(2) Click on the form that you want to open, in this case **Detailed Plant Form**.

(3) Click the **Open** button to display it.

(4) The selected form is displayed. If it is not sized correctly, you can maximize the display or resize the window to see as much of the form as needed.

For most users, the form is the most familiar method of entering or editing information. Everyone is comfortable using a form, and creating a form that is similar to a paper form you now use will eliminate many mistakes.

Task 18: Entering and Editing Information with a Form

Start Here

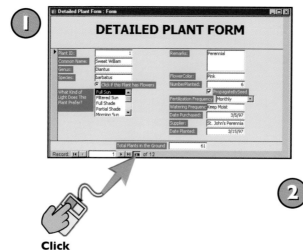
1

Click

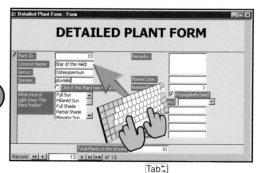
2
Tab⇥

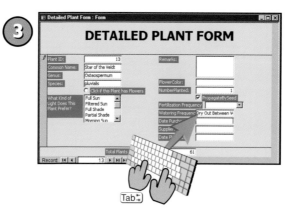
3
Tab⇥

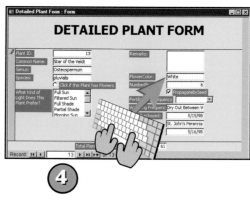
4

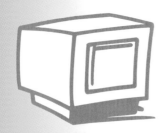

1 Before you can enter new information into a table, you must get to a blank record. Click the New Record button.

2 Press Tab to move to the **Common Name** field and type `Star of the Veldt`. Type `Osteospermum` in the Genus field and `pluvialis` in the Species field, pressing Tab after each.

3 Press Tab again. The cursor jumps to the **Watering Frequency** field. Type `Dry Out Between Watering`, and press Tab again.

4 Type `5/15/98` in the **Date Purchased** field; `St. John's Perennials` in **Supplier**; `5/16/98` in **Date Planted**; `White` in **FlowerColor**; `6` in **Number Planted**.

Next Step

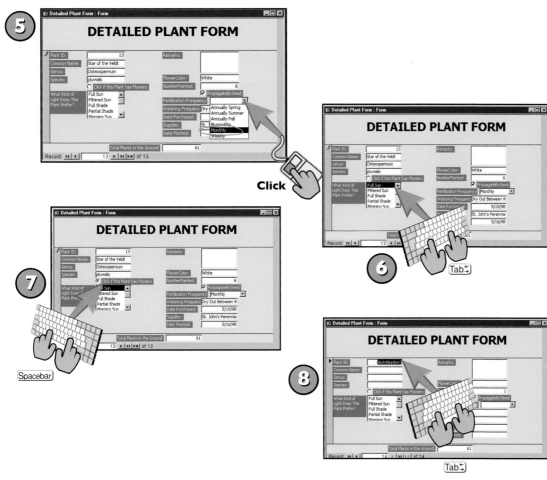

Click

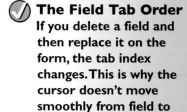

5 Press Tab twice, moving to the **Fertilization Frequency** field. Click the arrow button on the combo box and select **Monthly** from the list. Press Tab.

6 In the light preference list box, select the **Full Sun** option, and press Tab.

7 The cursor is now at the option button. Press the spacebar once to indicate that this plant does produce flowers.

8 Press the Tab key once more. A new blank record is displayed. You can enter a new record, and the one you just completed is automatically saved in the table.

✓ The Field Tab Order
If you delete a field and then replace it on the form, the tab index changes. This is why the cursor doesn't move smoothly from field to field.

End Task

Task 19: Changing the Field Order

The order in which the cursor moves from field to field on the form is called the tab index. In order for a form to work well, the cursor should move from one field to the next and not bounce around the screen.

The tab index is based on the order in which you placed a field on the form. You added all the fields once, but you also deleted several and then replaced them with other controls. This removed them from the tab index order and added them back at the end. Changing the tab index is easy.

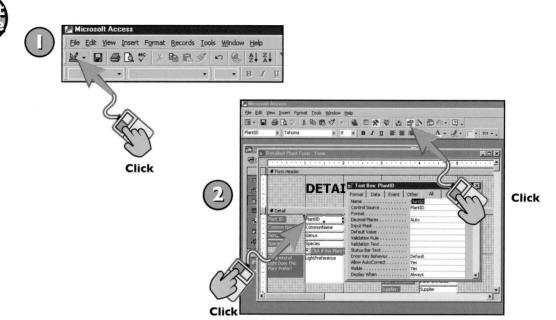

Click

Click

Click

Click

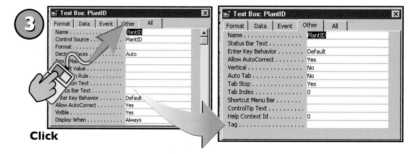

Click

1. Starting from the end of the previous task, click the View button to switch the form to Design view.

2. Select the **PlantID** field on your form, and click the Properties button.

3. Click the **Other** tab on the property sheet. This limits the display to only a few properties, including Tab Index and Tab Stop.

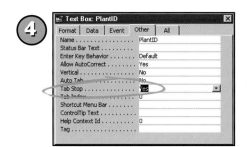

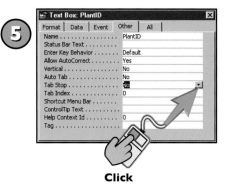

Click

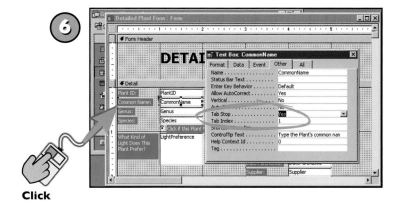

Click

The Tab Stop Property

The Tab Stop property determines whether the cursor stops at the field or passes it by. When set to No, the field is passed by when the Tab key is pressed. The first field placed on a form is always tab index 0.

Unique Tab Indexes

Access doesn't allow you to create duplicate tab index numbers. If you change tab index 13 to 3, the field that was tab index 3 would become 4, and so on.

(4) Move the cursor to the **Tab Stop** text box.

(5) Change the **Tab Stop** property from **Yes** to **No**.

(6) Select **CommonName** on the form to display its property sheet. The **Tab Stop** is **Yes**, and the **Tab Index** is **I**; leave these settings.

Changing the Field Order Continued

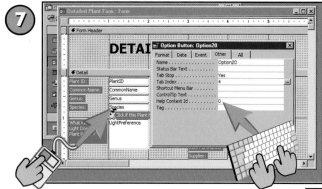

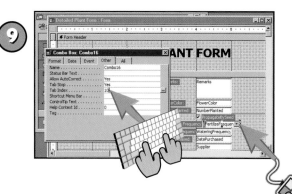

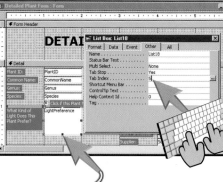

Click

Click

Click

Move the Property Sheet

If the property sheet is in the way, drag it from one side of the screen to the other so that it doesn't cover a field you need to select.

 Select each field in the order you want them selected when Tab is pressed. Check the tab index number for each field so that it is one greater than the previous. Change the Plant Flowers option button from 14 to 4.

 Change the **LightPreference** tab index from **14** to **5**.

 Change the tab index properties: Remarks, **6**; FlowerColor, **7**; NumberPlanted, **8**; PropagateBySeed, **9**; and FertilizeFrequency, **10**. Access adjusts the remaining fields.

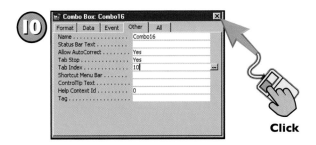

Click

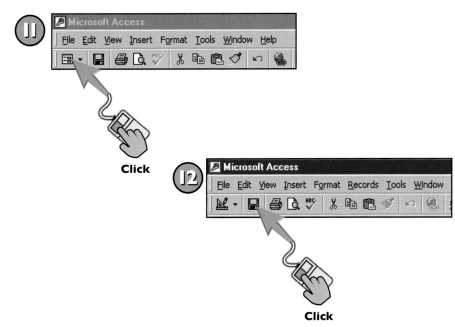

Click

Click

Close the Property Sheet by clicking X in the corner.

Click the View button and tab through a record to see if everything works as you expect.

Click the Save button to save the changes you have made.

End
Task

Getting Information from the Database

The capability to ask questions about the information in your database is one of the most powerful features in Access. A question is built in the form of an example and is called a *query*. Unlike a simple file in which you can look up one record at a time, Access can respond to a query by finding and displaying all records that meet certain *criteria*. Criteria are the set of restrictions that you place on what information is to be found—the *result set*.

There are several types of queries that you can use, each of which produces a different result. The following are the most commonly used:

- Select Query—Enables you to select and display a group of records. This will be a subset of the entire table; for example, all customers who live in the state of California.

- Crosstab Query—Use this query when you are sifting through a great deal of data looking for trends, or to generate summaries. You can also use this to create graphs about the data.

- Action Query—Use this query to add or update data in your table. For example, you can increase the selling price of all items now priced at $5 or more by 10 percent.

Like a table, a query can be used as the basis of a report or form. You can use queries to display information from several tables in a single form or report. When you first start creating your own queries, write them down. This will help you focus on the information you are looking for.

Tasks

Task #		Page #
1	Opening Query Design View	142
2	Running and Saving a Query	146
3	Adding Fields to the Query Grid	148
4	Selecting Records with Wildcards	152
5	Selecting Records with an OR Criterion	154
6	Selecting Records with More than One Criterion	156
7	Using Arithmetic Operators	158
8	Adding a New Field	160
9	Calculating a Value with a Query	161
10	Deleting Records with a Query	162
11	Creating a Query That Prompts for a Criteria Variable	166

Task 1: Opening Query Design View

The most common query that you will use is the select query. You can use it to choose records that meet the criteria you specify, and then display the result set in a datasheet (a table-like view). In this example, you will create a query for the statement "**Display all records for plants that have white flowers, including only the Common Name, Genus, Species, and Number Planted.**"

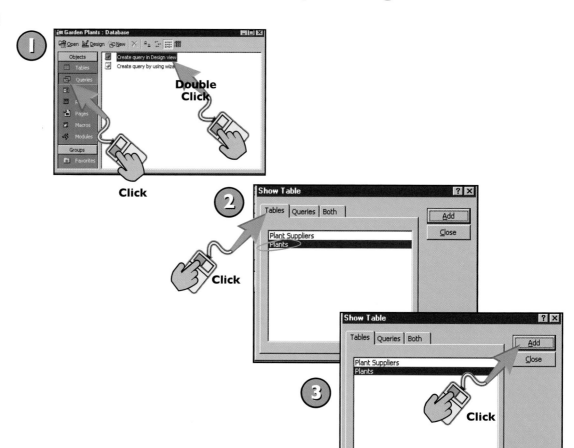

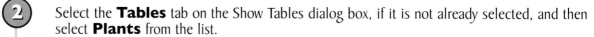

① In the open database, click the **Queries** button on the Database window. Double-click **Create query in Design view**. The Query Design view window and Show Table dialog box display.

② Select the **Tables** tab on the Show Tables dialog box, if it is not already selected, and then select **Plants** from the list.

③ Click the **Add** button to place it into the query Design view window.

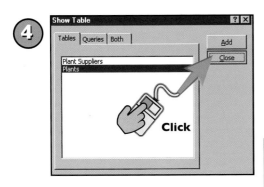

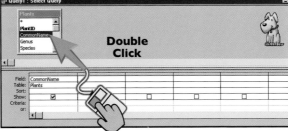

Double Click

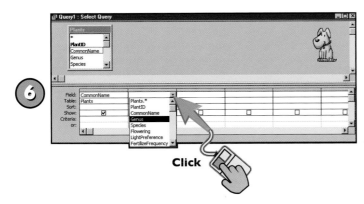

Click

✔ **The Asterisk and the Query Design Grid**
Select the asterisk to include all the fields in the table. It will automatically include any field added to the table later, or remove any field deleted from the table.

✔ **Scroll to View More Fields**
If you can't see a field on the query grid, use the horizontal scrollbar to see whether it is simply too far to the right to be seen. You can resize a column by dragging the right edge of any column selector button.

4 Click the **Close** button because this query is based on just this one table.

5 From the **Plants** field list box, double-click the **CommonName** field. Access immediately places the field on the query grid.

6 Click the mouse inside the **Field** row of the second column of the grid, and click the arrow button.

Opening Query Design View Continued

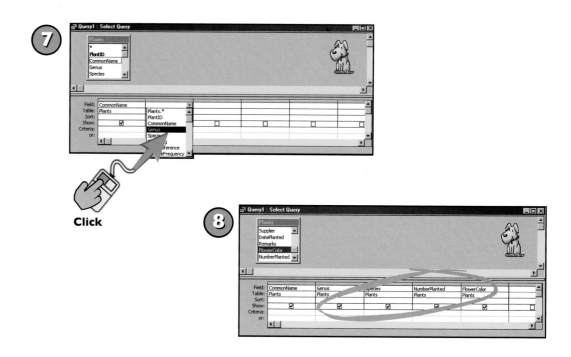

Click

⑦ Select **Genus** from the list as the second field for this query.

⑧ Add **Species**, **NumberPlanted**, and **FlowerColor** in the next three columns using either method.

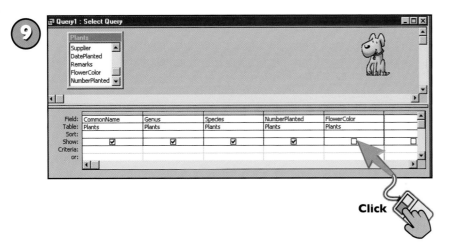

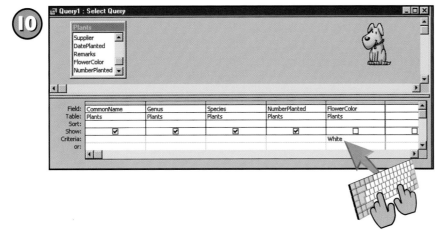

(9) Click the check box in the **Show** row of **FlowerColor**, removing the check mark so the field won't display in the result set. You can use a field as a criterion or for sorting but not show it.

(10) Click in the **Criteria** row of the **FlowerColor** column and type **White**. This is the actual criterion that a record must meet before it is included in the result set.

Task 2: Running and Saving a Query

After you have set up a query in the Query Design view grid, you can either run it or view the result set. For a select query, both of these terms mean the same thing. For any type of action query, *viewing* simply displays the records that the action will affect: These records will be updated, deleted, and so on. *Running* the query will actually apply the action to the selected records.

After you have created a query and it does what you expect of it, you can save it for later use. Saving a query is much easier than re-creating it later.

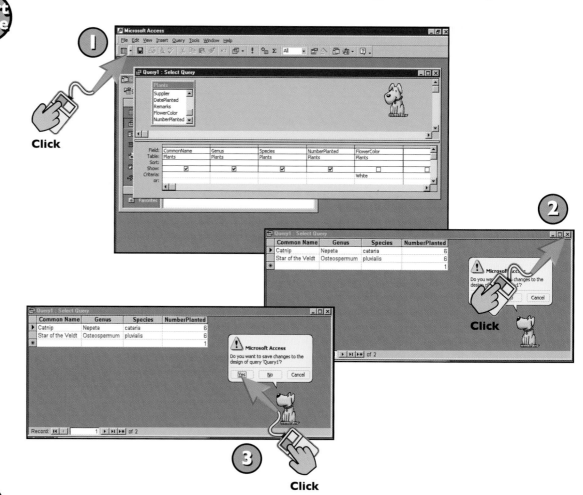

Start Here

Click

Click

Click

(1) Click the View button on the toolbar to see the result set for this query.

(2) Click the Close (**X**) button after you have viewed the results.

(3) The Office Assistant displays a balloon asking if you want to save this query. Click the **Yes** button.

Next Step

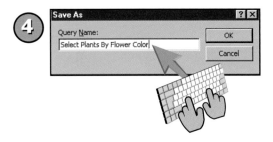

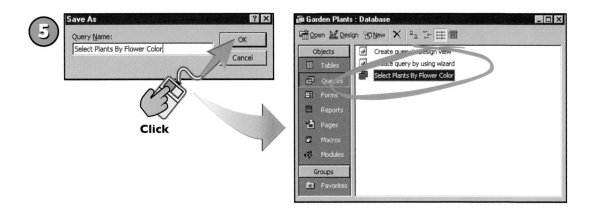

Click

4. In the Save As dialog box, type **Select Plants By Flower Color** in the **Query Name** text box.

5. Click **OK**. The new query is added to the Queries list in the Database window. You can easily reuse this query to find plants of another color by typing a different color criterion.

✔ **Reworking the Query**
If the query didn't perform as expected, simply click the View button again and return to Design view. Make any necessary adjustments, and then view the new result set.

Task 3: Adding Fields to the Query Grid

Start Here

Although using a table is an efficient method of storing information, it is rarely the best format for analyzing data. Access has a special query, called a *crosstab query*, designed specifically to help you summarize data. It can show values by comparing the data from one field to the data in another.

In this task, you will create a crosstab query to answer the query statement, "How many plants of each color have I planted?" This statement compares the number of plants you have by their color.

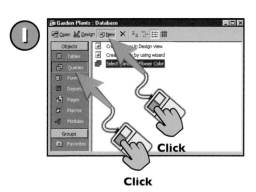

Click

Click

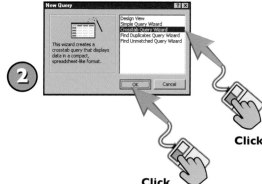

Click

Click

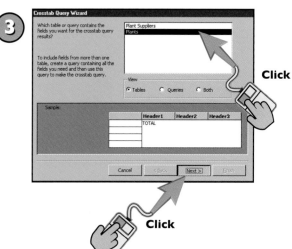

Click

Click

 Click the **Queries** tab button, and then the **New** button.

 Select **Crosstab Query Wizard** from the New Query dialog box, and then click **OK**.

Quick Open
You can quickly open the Crosstab Query Wizard by double-clicking the option in the New Query dialog box.

 The first Crosstab Query Wizard dialog box appears. Select the **Plants** table from the list, and then click the **Next>** button.

Next Step

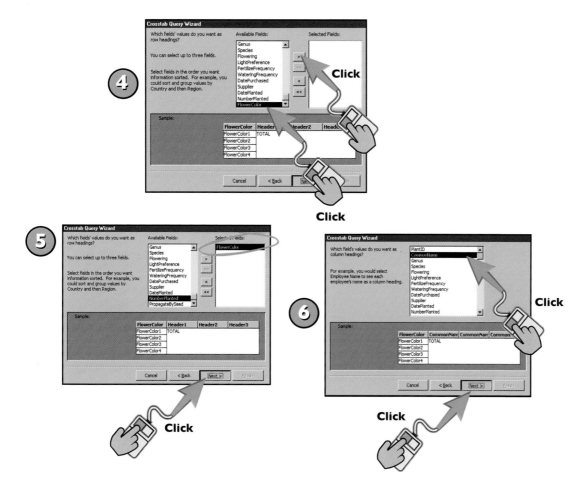

4   Choose **FlowerColor** as the comparison field by selecting it and then clicking the **>** button.

5   The field moves to the **Selected Fields** list. Click the **Next>** button.

6   Select **CommonName** as the field that will be used as the column heading. Click **Next>**.

✓ **Comparison Fields**
You can choose a maximum of three fields for your row headers, enabling you to sort and group fields.

Adding Fields to the Query Grid Continued

Click

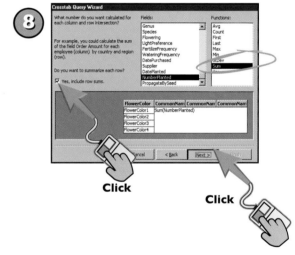

Click

Click

✓ The Result Set

The result set is displayed in a datasheet. Each of the various flower colors is listed in the first column, while the common name is shown as column titles. The second column, which shows the total number of plants in each color, is displayed as the second column. The first row has no color listed. If you look through the datasheet, you will see that Costmary has no color listed; either you didn't enter a color or the plant doesn't have a flower.

7 Choose a field that will be compared to the previously selected fields. Here you're comparing numbers of plants by color and name, so select **NumberPlanted**.

8 Choose the type of summary calculation you want—select the **Sum** function. Be sure to check the box **Yes, include row sums**, and then click **Next>**.

Next Step

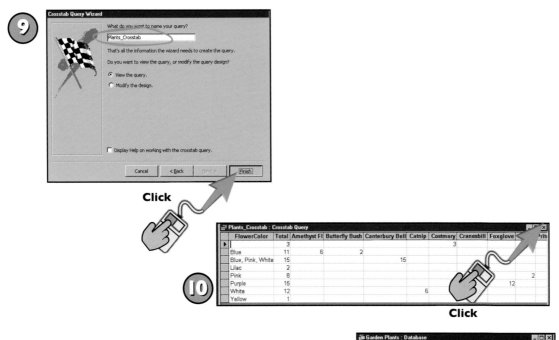

Click

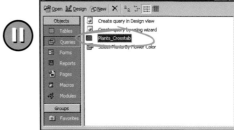

Click

9 Enter a title for the query—the default title is fine. Click the **Finish** button.

10 Click the Close (**X**) button.

11 Your Queries list appears. A query created with a wizard is automatically saved.

Task 4: Selecting Records with Wildcards

Sometimes when you want to search for information, you might not know exactly how something is spelled, or you might want to find all records that meet a partial criterion. For example, you might want to find all customers whose names begin with the letter B. Access gives you a set of wildcard characters that you can use in place of other letters.

The most common wildcard characters are the asterisk (*) and the question mark (?). An asterisk represents any number of any characters, and the question mark represents any single character.

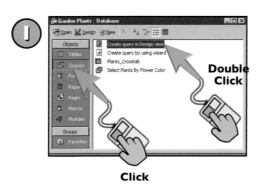

Click

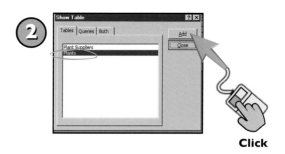

Double Click

Click

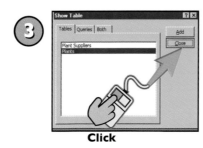

Click

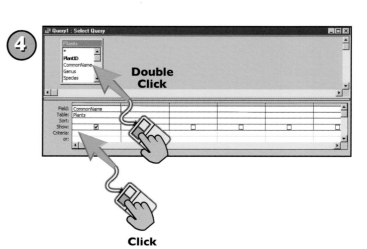

Double Click

Click

1. Click the **Queries** tab button, and then double-click the **Create query in Design view** option.

2. Select **Plants** from the Show Table dialog box, and then click **Add**.

3. Click the **Close** button.

4. Double-click the **CommonName** field. Move the cursor to the **Criteria** row of this same column.

Next Step

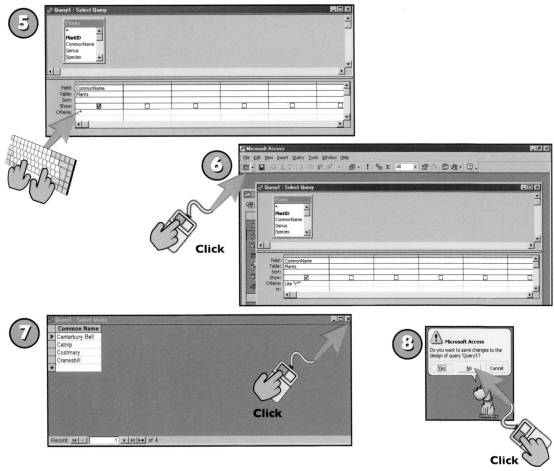

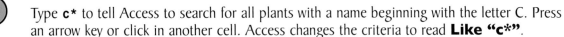

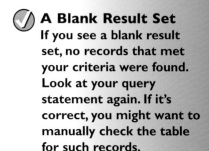

5 Type **c*** to tell Access to search for all plants with a name beginning with the letter C. Press an arrow key or click in another cell. Access changes the criteria to read **Like "c*"**.

6 Click the View button on the toolbar to see the result set.

7 Click the Close (**✕**) button.

8 When the Office Assistant prompts you to save the new query, select the **No** button.

✓ **A Blank Result Set**
If you see a blank result set, no records that met your criteria were found. Look at your query statement again. If it's correct, you might want to manually check the table for such records.

End Task

Task 5: Selecting Records with an OR Criterion

Often, you will want to find records that meet either one criterion or another. In this task, you want to find all plants that have either blue or white flowers. A query that says "Select this or select that" uses an **OR** operator, and tells Access to select any record that meets at least one of the criteria—it doesn't have to meet both.

OR criteria can be set up across multiple fields. For example, a query that asks "Select customers from the state of **NY** or from the city of **Los Angeles**" uses a multiple-field **OR** criterion.

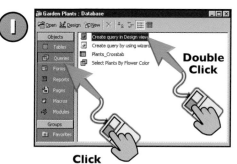

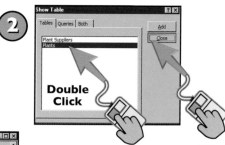

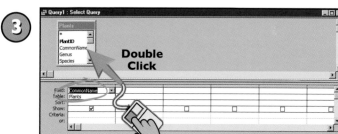

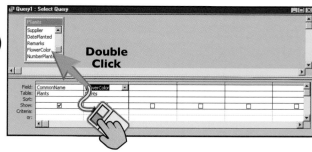

① Open the **Queries** list, then double-click the **Create query in Design view** option.

② Double-click the **Plants** table for this query, and then click the **Close** button.

③ Double-click the **CommonName** field to add it to the grid.

④ Double-click the **FlowerColor** field to add it to the grid.

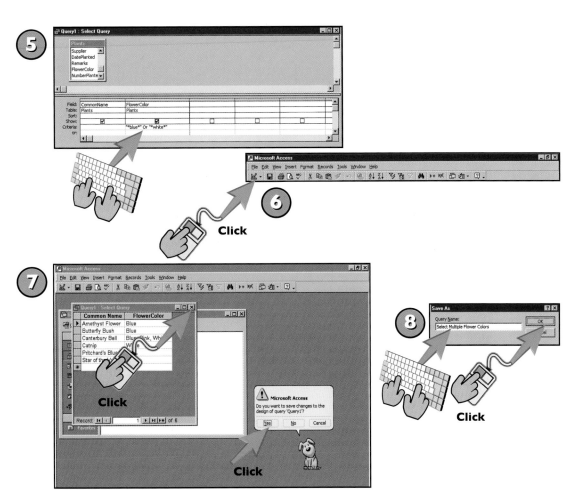

⑤ In the **Criteria** row of the **FlowerColor** column, type `"*blue*" OR "*white*"`, and then press the up-arrow key.

⑥ Click the View button to see the result set.

⑦ When you have viewed the result set, click the Close (**X**) button. Click the **Yes** button when prompted to save the query.

⑧ Type `Select Multiple Flower Colors` in the Save As dialog box, and then click **OK**.

Why Use Wildcards?
The asterisk wildcards ensure that plants with multiple flower colors will also be included.

One Line or Two
An OR criterion can be broken into two parts and placed in separate rows. The row below the **Criteria** row is labeled **or**. You can type the first criterion `"*blue*"` in the **Criteria** row, and then the second `"*white*"` in the next row.

Task 6: Selecting Records with More than One Criterion

Sometimes, you must find records that meet multiple criteria—for example, all customers who live in New York and who purchased blue widgets this year. For a customer to be included in the result set of this query, they must meet all criteria: living in New York, *and* having purchased blue widgets, *and* having made the purchase this year. This is an example of a query using an **AND** operator. In this task, you will use an **AND** operator to find all plants with blue flowers **AND** that require full sunlight.

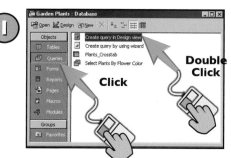

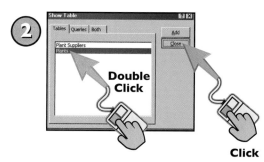

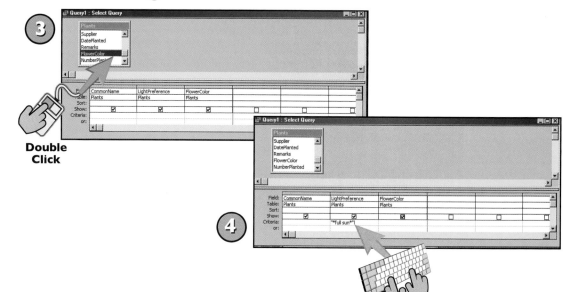

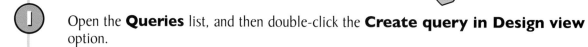

① Open the **Queries** list, and then double-click the **Create query in Design view** option.

② Double-click the **Plants** table for this query, and then click the **Close** button.

③ Double-click **CommonName**, **LightPreference**, and **FlowerColor** from the list box.

④ In the **Criteria** row of the **LightPreference** column, type `"*full sun*"`.

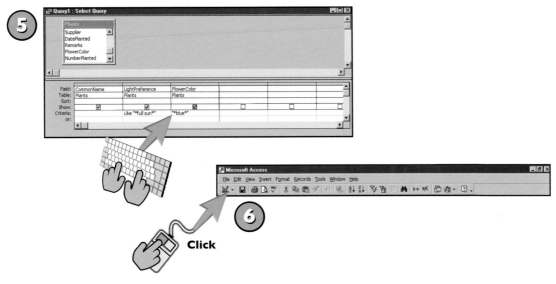

Click

Click

Click

✓ **AND and Criteria Rows**
You must enter the criteria in the same row for them to be considered an **AND** operator. Criteria entered in separate rows are considered to be **OR** criteria.

✓ **If There Are Extra Records**
If a result set includes records that don't meet both criteria you entered, click the View button and be sure that the criteria are not on different rows, accidentally creating an OR query instead.

5 In the **Criteria** row of the **FlowerColor** column, type "***blue***" and then click in another cell. Access adds **Like** to both criteria.

6 Click the View button to see the result set. Two records match the criteria. Notice the second record would be excluded without the wildcards in the color criteria.

7 Click the Close (**X**) button

8 Don't save the query when prompted by the Office Assistant—click **No**.

Task 7: Using Arithmetic Operators

The most commonly used arithmetic operators include equal (=), plus (+), less than (<), greater than (>), less than or equal to (<=), and greater than or equal to (>=). These operators can be used with text or numeric data. In contrast, these operators are used only with numeric information: minus (–), multiply (*), and divide (/). In this task, you will create a query that displays all plants with blue flowers that you planted on or after January 1, 1997.

Start Here

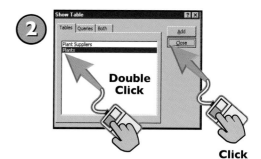

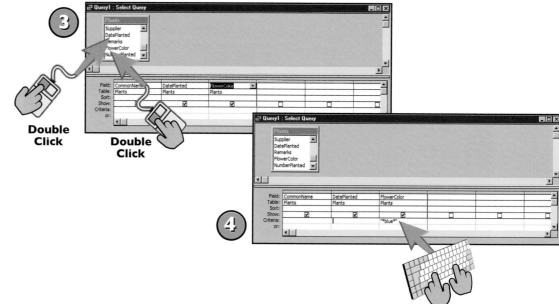

✔️ **An AND Operator**
Because this query requires the results to meet both criterion, the query uses an AND operator. Be sure you enter both criteria on the same row.

① Open the **Queries** list, then double-click the **Create query in Design view** option.

② Double-click the **Plants** table for this query, and then click the **Close** button.

③ From the Plants field list select **CommonName**, **DatePlanted**, and **FlowerColor**, placing each onto the query grid.

④ Move the cursor to the **Criteria** row in the **FlowerColor** column and type `"*blue*"` as the entry.

Next Step

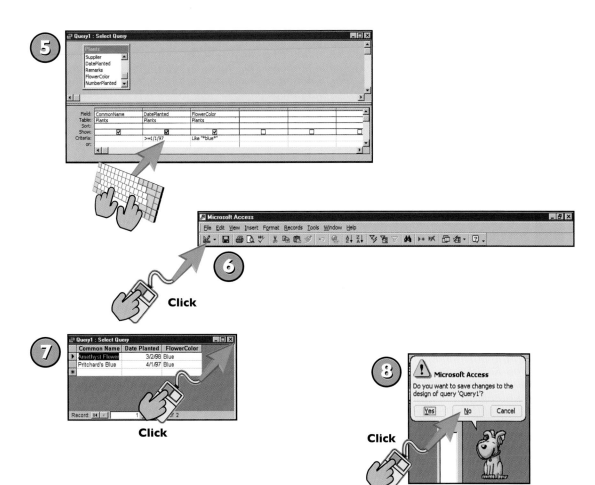

Click

Click

Click

✓ **Query Criteria**
If your query displays records that meet one or the other criterion, but not both, you have built an **OR** query by entering the criteria on separate lines. Make sure that the criteria statements are on the same line to create an **AND** query.

(5) Move the cursor to the **Criteria** row in the **DatePlanted** column, and type
>=1/1/97. Access changes this entry to read >=#1/1/97#.

(6) Click the View button to see the result set for this query.

✓ **The # Symbol**
In a query, the two # symbols indicate that the numbers between them are a date value.

(7) Close the datasheet.

(8) When prompted by the Office Assistant to save, click **No**.

Task 8: Adding a New Field

You can use a query to display fields that are not actually part of the underlying table. This is often done when you plan to use the query as the basis for a form or report. For example, in a report you might want to combine fields such as Last Name and First Name so that they will print together without a large space between them.

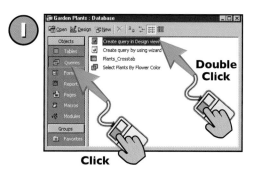

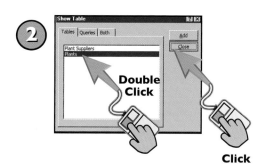

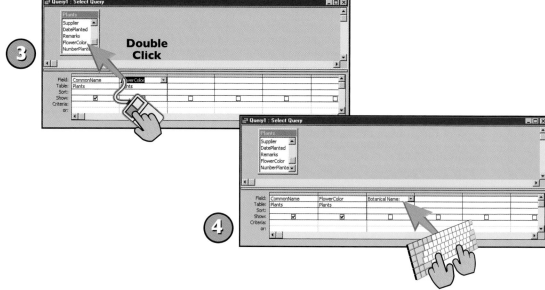

(1) Open the **Queries** list, and then double-click the **Create query in Design view** option.

(2) Double-click the **Plants** table for this query, and then click the **Close** button.

(3) Select the **CommonName** and **FlowerColor** fields, and place them onto the query grid.

(4) Move the cursor to the blank column beside **FlowerColor** on the grid, in the **Field** row, and type **Botanical Name:**—be sure to end with the colon (:).

Task 9: Calculating a Value with a Query

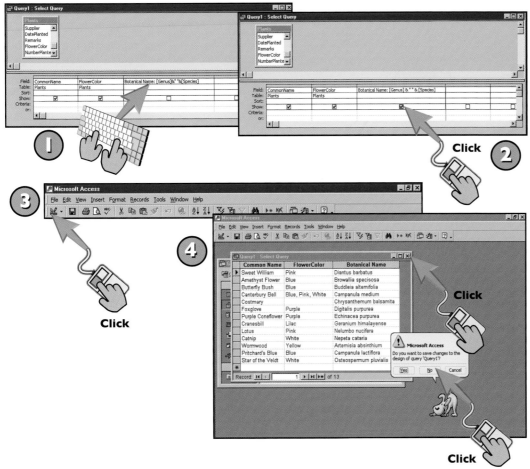

Click **2**

Click

Click **4**

Click

Click

A calculated field can manipulate values from numeric or text fields. You can calculate two numeric values like this: **Extended Price: [Quantity] * [SellPrice].** A new field named Extended Price is created and displays the total from multiplying the number in the Quantity field by that in the SellPrice field.

✓ **Additional Calculated Field Examples**
You can also combine text fields like this: **Customer Name: [FirstName]&" "&[LastName].** This example creates a new field called **Customer Name** filled with the values from the FirstName and LastName fields. The ampersand (&) adds the fields together. Between the two ampersands is a space surrounded by double quote marks. This gives you the single space between the customer's first and last names. A calculated field like this example is not normally saved in a table.

1 In the newly created **Botanical Name:** field from Task 8, create a calculation by typing **[Genus]&" "&[Species]**; be sure to leave a space between the quote marks.

2 Click in the **Show** check box so that the new field is displayed in the result set.

3 Click the View button to see the result set.

4 Click the Close (**X**) button, and then the **No** button when prompted to save the new query.

Task 10: Deleting Records with a Query

You can create an action query that will delete unwanted records. You can delete records one by one, but if you must remove many records and they can be ferreted out using criteria, you can use a delete query. In order for this to be worth the time and effort, the records must be selectable as a group. For example, you could create a query that would delete all customer records for those customers who have not purchased products in the last three years. This is a selectable group of records.

Start Here

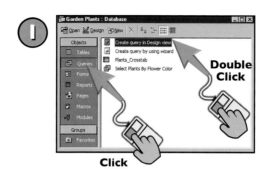
Double Click

Click

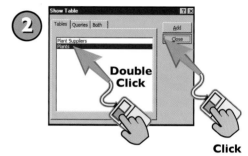
Double Click

Click

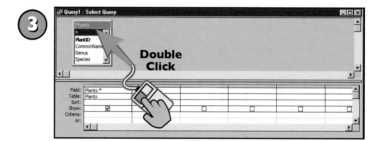
Double Click

Open the **Queries** list, then double-click the **Create query in Design view** option.

Double-click the **Plants** table for this query, and then click the **Close** button.

Double-click the * (asterisk) in the Plants field list. This automatically includes all fields contained in the table.

Next Step

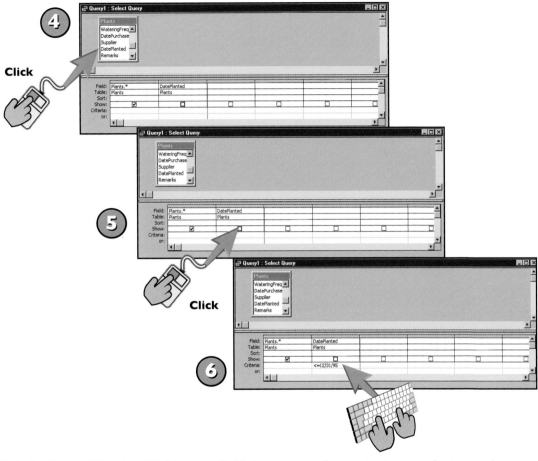

Click

Click

④ Click the **DatePlanted** field as the field that you use for a criterion to select records.

⑤ Remove the check mark so that this field doesn't appear twice in the result set.

⑥ In the **Criteria** row of the **DatePlanted** column, type **<=12/31/95**. This will select all records that were planted on or before December 31, 1995.

Deleting Records with a Query
Continued

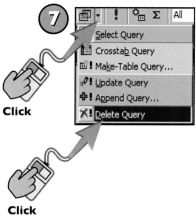

Click

Click

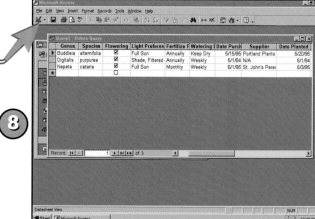

Click 8

✓ Running an Action Query

The records will be deleted if you click the Run button on the Query Design view toolbar. You can also run a saved action query any time by selecting it in the Database window.

 7 Click the down-arrow part of the Query Type button on the toolbar, and select **Delete Query** from the list. This is an action query.

 8 Click the View button to see that three records are selected by the query.

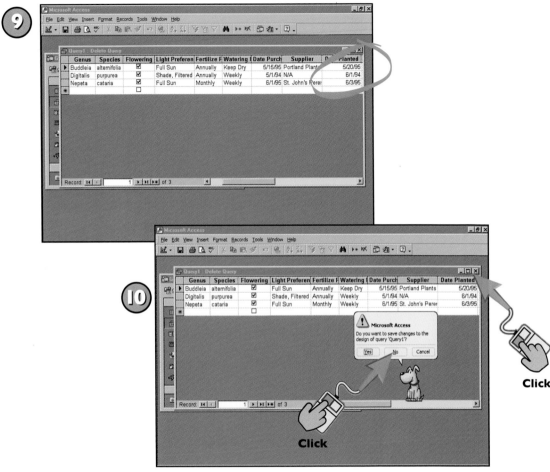

⑨ Scroll to the **DatePlanted** column to verify that these records do meet the criteria.

⑩ Click the Close (**X**) button and don't save the query.

Sometimes you will create a query for a single purpose, but later decide that you want to use it again with slightly different criteria. For example, earlier you created the "Select Plants By Flower Color" query that displayed all plants with white flowers. If you want to use this query to find plants with blue flowers, you can edit the query and change the criteria from white to blue. Alternatively, you can change the criteria to always prompt you for the color that you want to find—this is called a *parameter* query.

Task 11: Creating a Query That Prompts for a Criteria Variable

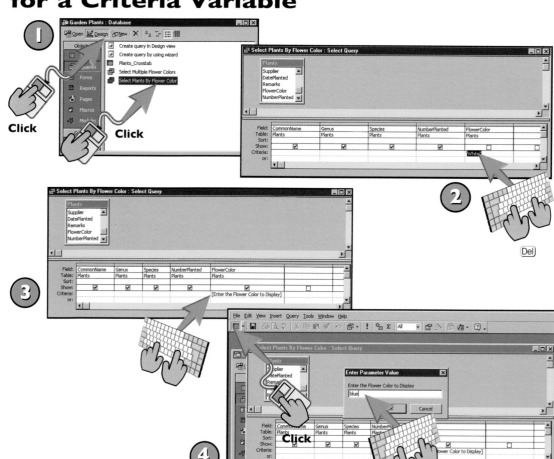

In the Queries window, click on the **Select Plants By Flower Color** query, and then click the **Design** button.

Select the criterion **"white"**, and press the Delete key.

Type **[Enter the Flower Color to Display]**. Be sure that the check box in this column is checked.

Click the View button, and then type **blue** in the Parameter dialog box that displays.

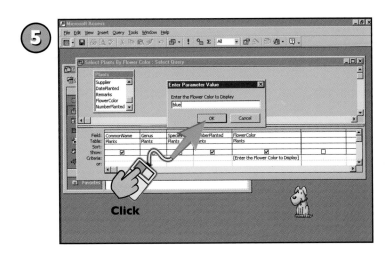

Click

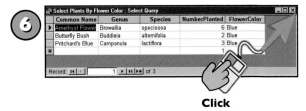

Click

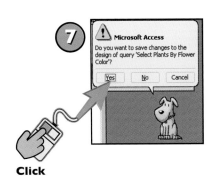

Click

5 Click **OK** to view the result set.

6 Click the Close (**X**) button.

7 Click **Yes** when prompted to save the changes to the query.

Creating and Using Reports

Although you can print copies of tables, forms, and query data sheets, you have much greater control over the format when it is printed as a report. Many of the techniques you learned for building a form can be used to create a report. With a report, you will also learn to group records and create summary information such as totals, subtotals, and percentages. Summary data can be shown for groups of records and for the report as a whole.

Reports are often based on queries rather than tables. This lets you select only the records that will be included, instead of automatically reporting on all records. When you use a query as the basis of the report, the query is run when you access the report, and then the report is displayed or printed.

You can create reports for mailing labels, invoices, product tags, address and phone lists, sales and purchase analysis, sales contacts, and any other information that you store in a table.

Tasks

Task #		Page #
1	Building a Report with a Wizard	170
2	Opening the Report Design View	176
3	Adding Fields to the Report	177
4	Using Titles	178
5	Adding Automatic Page Numbers and Dates	180
6	Grouping Records	182
7	Sorting Records	184
8	Moving Field Labels on the Report	186
9	Moving Fields on the Report	188
10	Using Calculated Fields in a Report	192
11	Adding Special Effects to a Report	196
12	Viewing a Report	200
13	Saving a Report	202
14	Printing a Report	203

Task 1: Building a Report with a Wizard

You have learned to use tables to store information, you have created forms to work with the data, and you have learned to use queries to search for specific information. Suddenly, your boss wants a report on her desk by quitting time today. What should you do?
By using the Report Wizard, you can quickly create a report that has a polished, professional appearance. You have a choice of several styles for the layout and how records will be grouped.

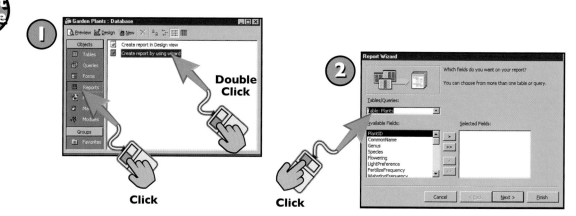

Double
Click

Click

Click

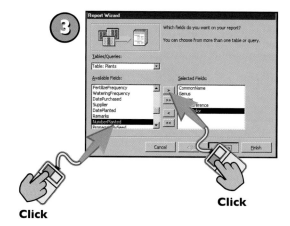

Click

Click

1. Click the **Reports** objects button on the Database window, and then double-click the **Create report by using wizard** option.

2. Select **Table: Plants** in the Tables/Queries combo box.

3. Select the fields **CommonName**, **Genus**, **Species**, **LightPreference**, and **FlowerColor** for the report by clicking the **>** button after each selection.

Next
Step

Task 3: Adding Fields to the Report

Start Here

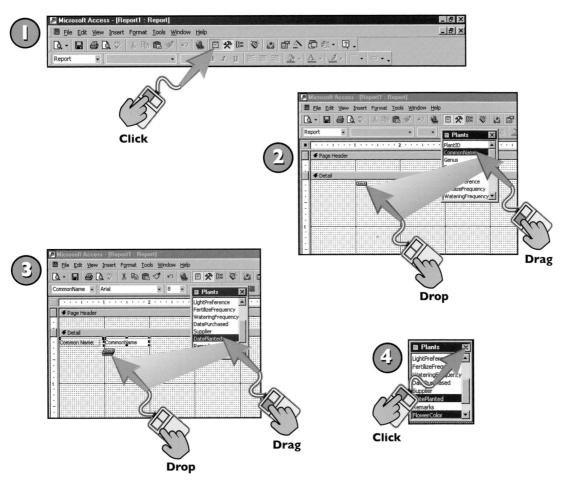

Click

Drag

Drop

Drag

Drop

Click

You must add fields to a report so that some sort of information is displayed. As with forms, fields placed on a report display the data from the table or query on which the report is based. Also like a form, fields are placed with both a field and label part, both of which can be moved independently of the other.

① Click the Field List button on the toolbar to open the Field List box.

② Select the **CommonName** field from the list and drag it from the box to the Detail grid. The Detail grid is the large area below the bar labeled **Detail**.

③ Now drag and drop the fields **Genus**, **Species**, **DatePlanted**, and **FlowerColor** onto the detail grid below the **CommonName** field.

④ Close the Field list by clicking its Close (**X**) button.

✓ **Closing the Field List Box**
When the Field List box is displayed in the Design view window, you can close it by clicking the Field List button on the toolbar.

End Task

Task 4: Using Titles

Start Here

Titles are used even more extensively in reports than in forms. Report titles are usually of two types: Report titles that are printed once per report, and page titles that are printed on each page.

Titles are usually placed in either the **Report Header** or the **Page Header** grid, depending on whether you want it to be displayed once or on every page. A new report always includes a page header but not a report header.

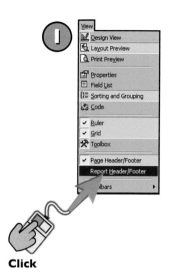
Click

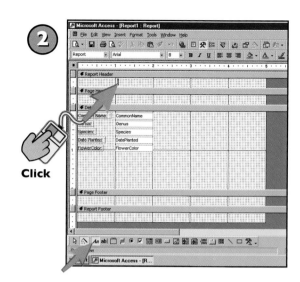
Click

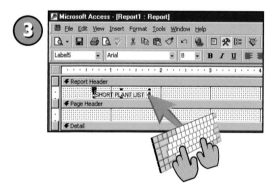

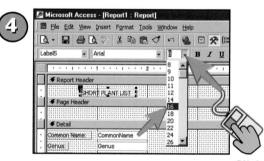
Click

 Select **View**, **Report Header/Footer** from the menu. You'll see two new grid sections added to the Design view window, the Report Header and Report Footer.

 Click the Label button on the toolbox, then move the mouse to the Report Header grid and click once. A very small text box is placed where you clicked.

 Type **SHORT PLANT LIST** and press Enter to select the label box. Notice how Access automatically increases the size of the box as you type.

 Click the arrow on the Font Size button and choose **16** as the new font size for this label.

Next Step

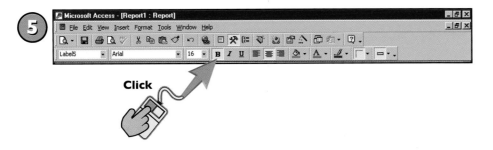

Click

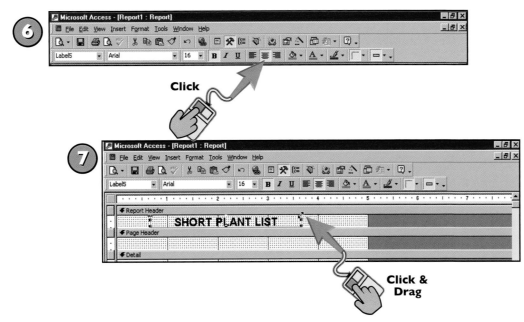

Click

Click & Drag

5 Click the Bold button.

6 Click the Center button.

7 Increase the size of the label box by dragging handles until all the text is visible.

End Task

Task 5: Adding Automatic Page Numbers and Dates

Access can automatically add page numbers and the date and time. You can choose where these will be placed—in the header or footer—and some of the formatting for the item. You can also edit the format of any of them.

Start Here

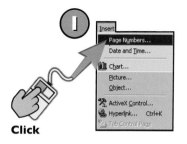
Insert
Page Numbers...
Date and Time...
Chart...
Picture...
Object...
ActiveX Control...
Hyperlink...   Ctrl+K
Tab Control Page
Click

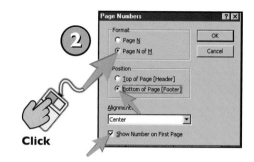
Page Numbers
Format
Page N
Page N of M
Position
Top of Page [Header]
Bottom of Page [Footer]
Alignment:
Center
Show Number on First Page
OK
Cancel
Click

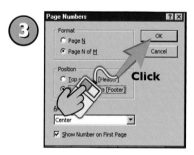
Page Numbers
Format
Page N
Page N of M
Position
Top [Header]
[Footer]
Center
Show Number on First Page
OK
Cancel
Click

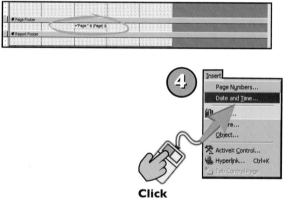
Page Footer
"Page " & [Page] &
Report Footer

Insert
Page Numbers...
Date and Time...
Object...
ActiveX Control...
Hyperlink...   Ctrl+K
Tab Control Page
Click

(1) Add automatic page numbering by clicking **Insert**, **Page Numbers**. The Page Numbers dialog box appears.

(2) Click the **Page N of M** and **Bottom of Page** options, and **Center** for the Alignment. Be sure that the **Show Number on First Page** check box is checked.

(3) Click **OK**. Notice the new text box placed in the Page Footer grid. This will print on every page of the report.

(4) Click **Insert**, **Date and Time** from the menu to open the Date and Time dialog box.

Next Step

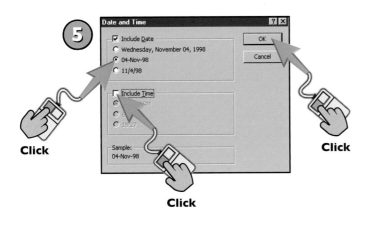

5 Click

Click

Click

6

Click

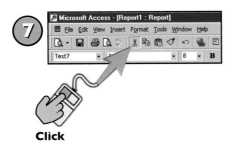

7

Click

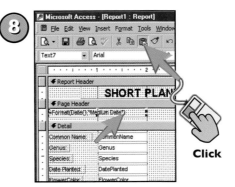

8

Click

5 Click the second option button in the **Include Date** group. Uncheck the **Include Time** check box. Click **OK**.

6 You will see the new date text box has been placed in the upper-left corner of the Report Header grid. Click on the new date text box to select it.

7 Click the Cut button on the toolbar to remove the new date text box from the Report Header grid.

8 Click anywhere inside the Page Header grid, and then click the Paste button on the toolbar to set the date on each page of the report.

✓ **Date and Time Examples**
The sample date and times you see on your screen might be different than shown. They're automatically generated formats taken from your computer settings.

✓ **Cut and Paste Shortcut**
You can also cut a selected object by pressing Ctrl+X, and then paste it by pressing Ctrl+V.

Task 6: Grouping Records

You can group records in a report instead of simply printing them in the order they appear in the table or query. Grouping records is a simple way to organize your information. For example, if you were creating a sales report, you might want to group information by region, and then subdivide regions by sales person. This is a two-level grouping.

Groups not only organize your report; you can also create summary calculations for groups as you can for an entire report.

 The Yes Property
You use the Group grid to place information about the group. Leaving these properties set to No allows you to sort records by the group field without it printing on the report.

Click

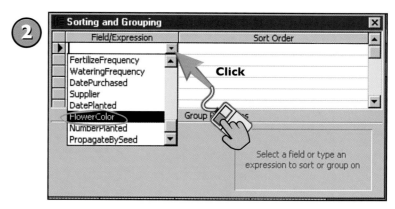

Click

 Click the **Sorting and Grouping** button on the toolbar to open the Sorting and Grouping dialog box.

Click the first column and row of the Sorting and Grouping dialog box, then the down arrow button displayed. Choose the **FlowerColor** field from the drop-down list.

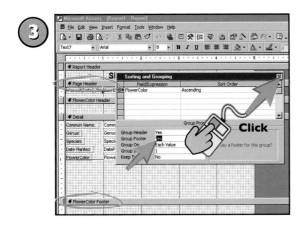

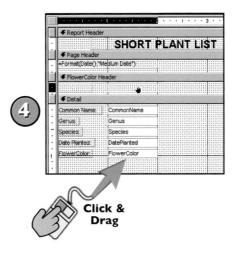

Click & Drag

③ Select **Yes** for both **Group Header** and **Group Footer** in the **Group Properties** section. This creates a group grid on your report. Click the Close (**X**) button.

④ Select and drag and drop the **FlowerColor** field object from the detail grid to the FlowerColor Header grid. Be sure to drag the field object and not the label.

Task 7: Sorting Records

In addition to grouping records, you can also sort records. A report with its information sorted into a recognizable format is much easier to read than one in which the information is simply placed haphazardly into the report.
Groups are always sorted, and you can sort by additional fields within the group.

Start Here

Click

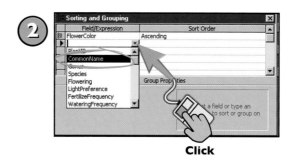

Click

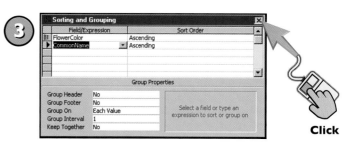

Click

 Click the Sorting and Grouping button to display its dialog box.

 Click the arrow button in the second row and select **CommonName**. Within each FlowerColor group the records will be sorted by common name in ascending order.

 Close the Sorting and Grouping dialog box by clicking its Close (**X**) button.

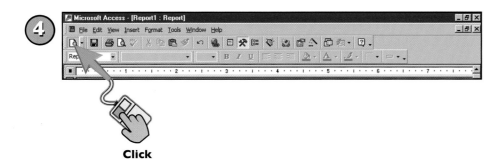

Click

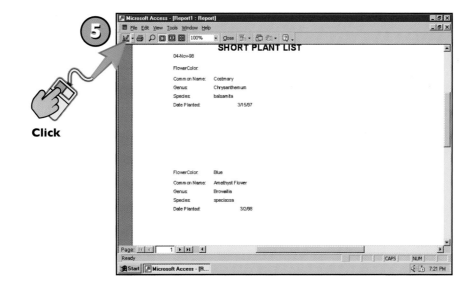

Click

 To see what your report currently looks like, click the View button.

 Click the View button again to return to the Design view window.

Task 8: Moving Field Labels on the Report

When you create a report in Access, field labels are included for each field that you place on the report. This means that you have a label for each field in the detail section. This becomes quite crowded and repetitive on paper. One way to eliminate this confusion is to move the detail record labels from beside its field to a group or page header. In this task, you will move the detail record labels to the FlowerColor group.

✓ **Moving Labels**
Be careful to align the labels with the data they describe. You don't want someone to misread your report because a label is not aligned with its field.

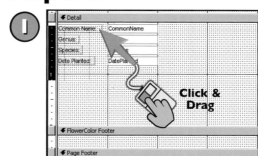

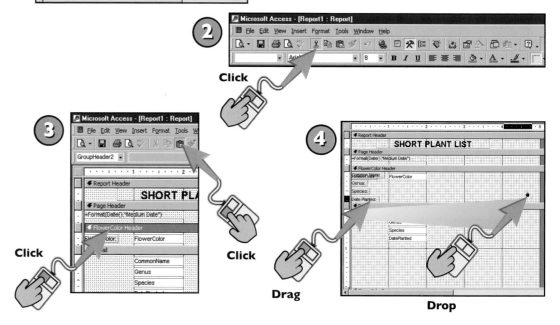

1. Select all the detail record field labels by dragging a selection box around them. Be sure not to include any of the fields.

2. Click the Cut button on the toolbar.

3. Click anywhere on the **FlowerColor Header** grid and click the Paste button.

4. Click anywhere in the **FlowerColor Header** area to deselect the four labels, and then click on and drag the **Date Planted** label.

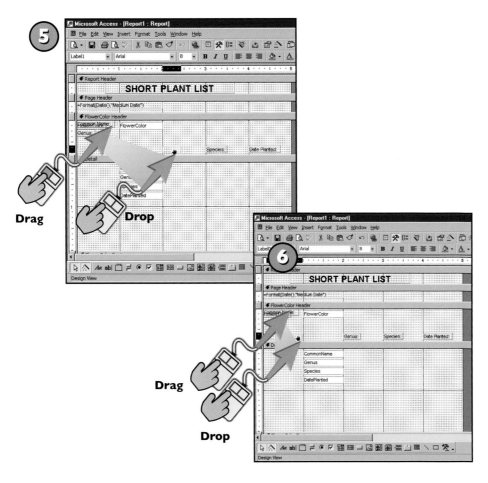

5 Drag the other two visible labels so that they are to the left of the Date Planted label.

6 **Common Name** is the last label and might be difficult to get to. It is on top of the Flower Color label, but is a little longer. Simply click its right edge and then drag it down.

Task 9: Moving Fields on the Report

Start
Here

After you have moved the field labels so that they are in a horizontal rather than a vertical group, you will want to shift the fields so that they are in line with their own labels.

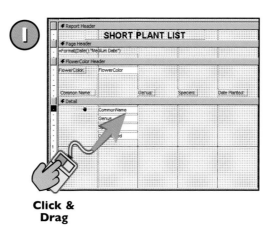

Click & Drag

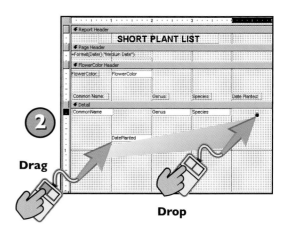

Drag

Drop

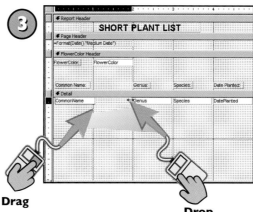

Drag

Drop

1. Click on the **CommonName** field object and drag it to the left side and to the top of the Detail grid.

2. Select and drag each remaining field so it is directly beneath its label in the FlowerColor Header grid, but keep it in the Detail grid area.

3. Some common names are rather long, so click on and drag the right edge of the **CommonName** field so that it is next to the Genus field.

Next
Step

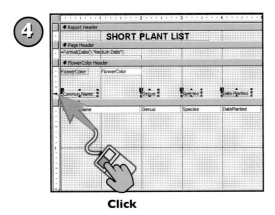

Click

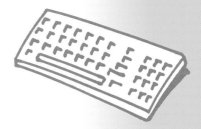

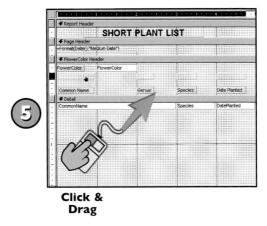

**Click &
Drag**

④ Move the mouse to the vertical ruler beside the field labels in the FlowerColor Header and click once to select all the labels.

⑤ Drag the labels up and drop them beneath the **FlowerColor** label and field.

Moving Fields on the Report Continued

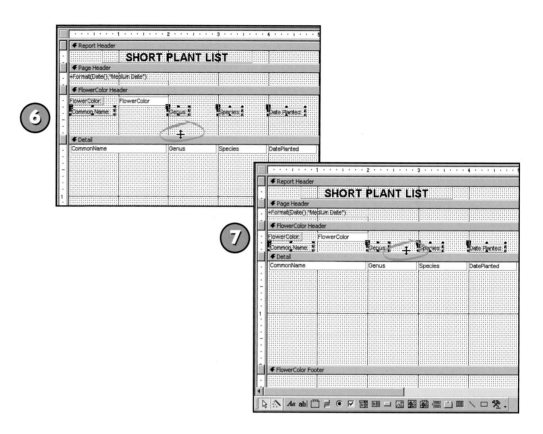

6. Move the mouse pointer to the top edge of the Detail bar so that the pointer changes shape to a pair of up and down arrows and a horizontal bar.

7. Drag the bar up until it touches the detail field labels, decreasing the size of the FlowerColor Header grid.

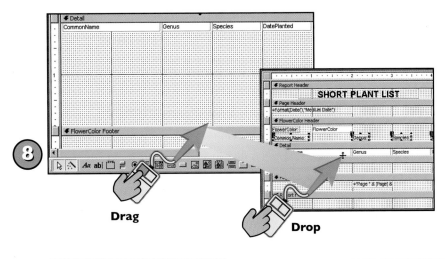

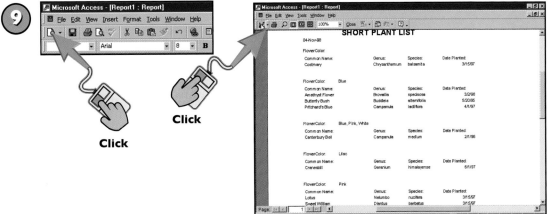

Drag

Drop

Click

Click

Click

8 Do the same at the top edge of the **FlowerColor Footer** bar, dragging it up snug against the field objects.

9 Click the View button to see the current report. Return to Design view by clicking the View button once again.

Task 10: Using Calculated Fields in a Report

You can use calculated fields in reports for many of the same reasons that you use them in forms. You can calculate values that are not included in a table, or combine information from multiple fields so that a report is easier to read. Calculated fields can also be used for summary information for groups, pages, or the entire report. In this task, you will delete the Genus and Species fields and labels and replace them with a calculated text field.

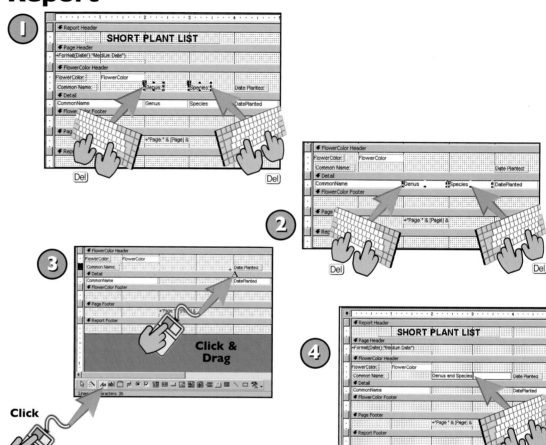

① Select both the **Genus** and **Species** labels on the FlowerColor Header grid and press the Delete key.

② Select and delete both the **Genus** and **Species** field objects on the Detail grid.

③ Click the Label button on the toolbox and drag a new label to the place you deleted the labels in the FlowerColor header.

④ Type **Genus and Species** into the label.

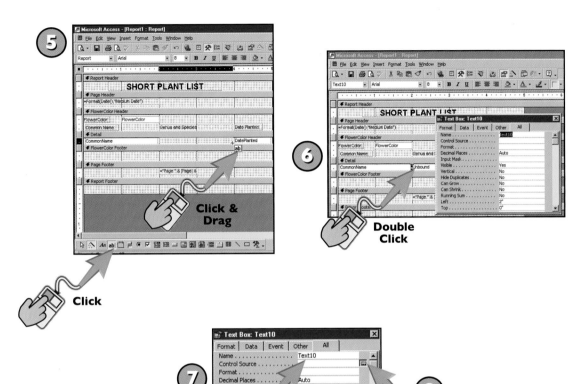

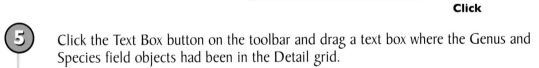

5   Click the Text Box button on the toolbar and drag a text box where the Genus and Species field objects had been in the Detail grid.

6   Select and delete the new text box's label. Double-click the new **Unbound** text box, displaying its property sheet.

7   Click the **Control Source** combo box.

8   Click the Build (**...**) button beside it to display the Expression Builder dialog box.

Using Calculated Fields in a Report Continued

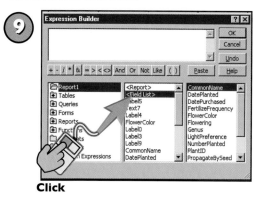

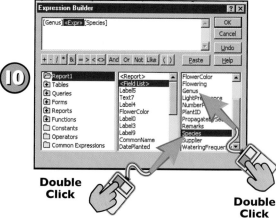

Click

Double Click

Double Click

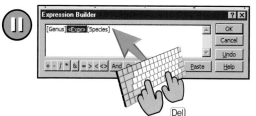

Del

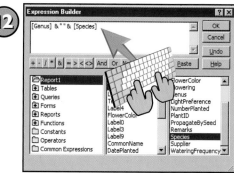

(9) In the middle list box click the **<Field List>** option to display the list of all available fields in the right list box.

(10) Double-click both the **Genus** and **Species** fields in the list.

(11) Select and delete the **Expr** between the two fields in the expression text box.

(12) Between the two fields type **&** " " **&** to link these two as a calculated text field.

Next Step

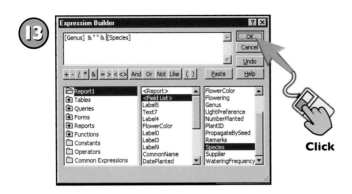

13

Click

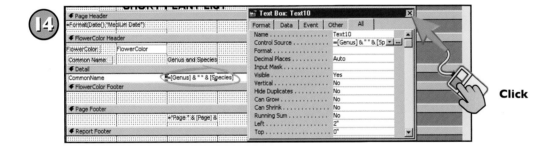

14

Click

13 Click **OK** on the Expression Builder dialog box. You will see the new formula entered into the Control Source combo box.

14 Close the property sheet and you will see the formula also in the text box.

Task 11: Adding Special Effects to a Report

There are several special effects that you can use on a report. You can draw lines or boxes; use color, shade, or shadows; or change the color of a font. Although there are many things that you can do, don't go totally wild. Always remember what type of printer you will be using. If you are using a laser printer, color will not show up except as patterns and shades of gray. Some colored objects can appear very muddied and hard to read. Also, too much color, even when printed on a color printer, can cause a report to print very slowly.

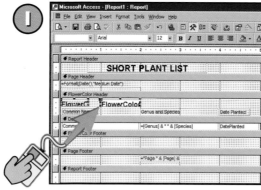

Start Here

1

Click

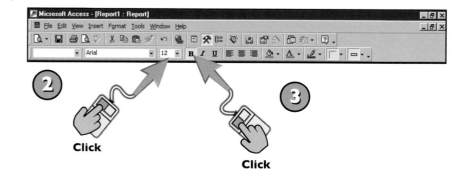

2 **Click**

3 **Click**

1 Select the **FlowerColor** field object and label.

2 Increase the font size from **8** to **12**.

3 Click the Bold button.

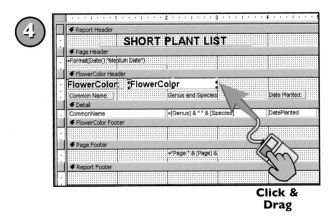

**Click &
Drag**

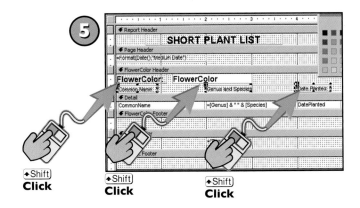

◆Shift
Click

◆Shift
Click

◆Shift
Click

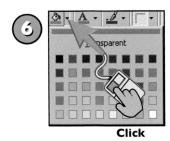

Click

(4) Increase the size of both objects so that all the text is displayed.

(5) Select the three detail field labels in the FlowerColor Header.

(6) Click the down-arrow button beside the Fill/Back Color button to display its pallet box.

Adding Special Effects to a Report Continued

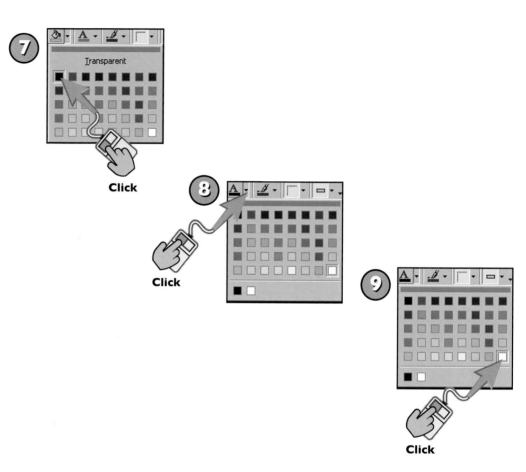

Click

Click

Click

⑦ Select the Black color box in the upper-left corner.

⑧ Click the down-arrow button beside the Font/Fore Color button, displaying its pallet box.

⑨ Click the White color box in the lower-right corner.

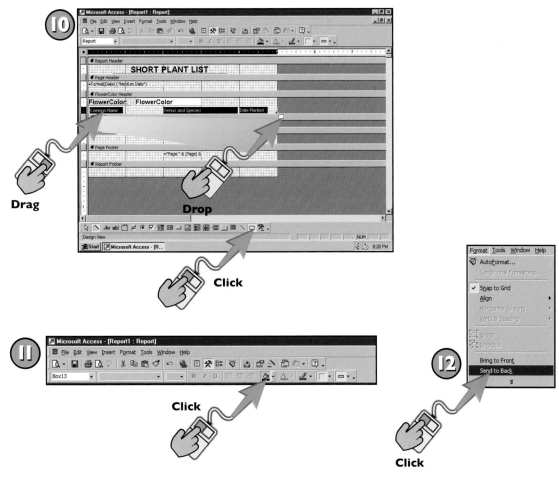

Drag

Drop

Click

Click

Click

Click the Box tool on the toolbox and drag a box around the three labels. When you release the mouse button you will see a box over the labels.

Click the Fill/Back Color button. This will change the box color to black, which was the last color selected.

You still can't see the labels. Click **Format**, **Send to Back** from the menu.

Task 12: Viewing a Report

Before you complete a report, especially when you design a new report, you should view it. Look for formatting problems such as whether the text is all bunched on one side of the page, whether labels and fields are aligned properly, whether too much space exists between elements of the report, and whether the font size and type are appropriate to the subject. If you have used summary calculations in a footer, be sure they are properly labeled and aligned beneath the fields that they are summarizing. Sometimes you might need to make number fields smaller in a report in order to align them where you want them.

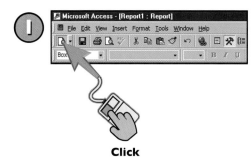

Click

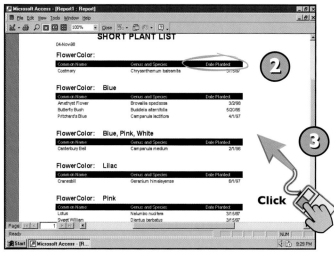

Click

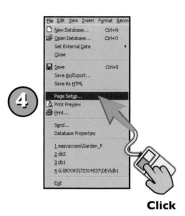

Click

Click the View button on the toolbar.

In this view, look at field labels and detail records. Are they well aligned? The label **Date Planted** could be moved to the right.

When looking at a 100% view you might not see page formatting problems. Click the mouse to shrink the page. In this view you can see that the report text is not centered on the page.

Click **File**, **Page Setup** from the menu to display the Page Setup dialog box.

Next Step

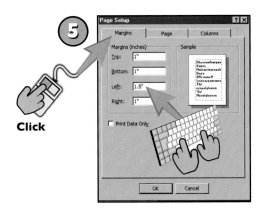

Click

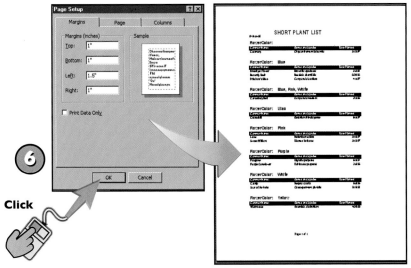

SHORT PLANT LIST

Click

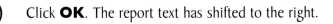

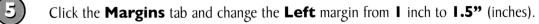

5 Click the **Margins** tab and change the **Left** margin from **1** inch to **1.5"** (inches).

6 Click **OK**. The report text has shifted to the right.

Task 13: Saving a Report

After you have created a report that you want to use, you must save it just like any other Access object that you have created. After it is saved, you can use it over and over simply by clicking it from the **Reports** tab on the Database window.

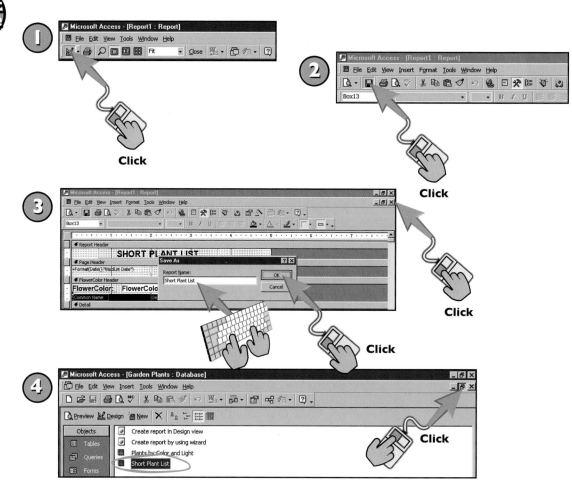

Start Here

Click

Click

Click

Click

Click

(1) Click the View button to return to the Design view window.

(2) Click the Save button on the toolbar.

(3) Type **Short Plant List** and then click **OK**. Click the Close (**X**) button on the Design view window

(4) Click the Restore button on the Database window. You will see your new report listed on the Reports tab.

End Task

Task 14: Printing a Report

Start Here

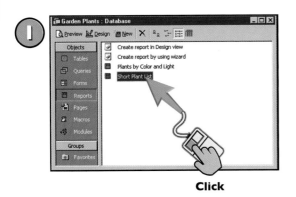

Click

Click

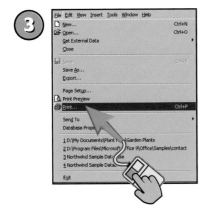

Click

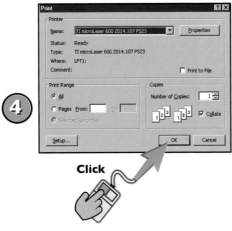

Click

In order to easily share a report with others, you must print it. Although you can view a report onscreen, as you have already done in the Report Preview mode, this is not the easiest way for several people to see the report.

① Select the **Short Plant List** report in the **Reports** tab list.

② Click the Print button on the toolbar. When you print this way, you do not have the option to specify numbers of copies or a printer other than the default printer.

③ To make additional choices when printing a report, select **File**, **Print** from the menu to display the Print dialog box.

④ Make any necessary changes, and click **OK** to print.

End Task

7

Advanced Features

In this part, you will learn to combine information from multiple databases and tables. By combining information from several tables, you can query the information within the databases, which is then used as the basis for a form or report. These forms and reports provide more valuable and useful information. You will do this by creating relationships between tables by using primary and foreign key fields.

Next, sharing this information is important. You will learn to import and export information to and from other programs and to create a simple Web page from data contained in your database. You also will be working with Data Access Pages, a new feature of Access 2000 that enables users to access, add, and edit information in a database.

Tasks

Task #		Page #
1	Building Permanent Relationships	206
2	Using a Query with Multiple Tables	208
3	Creating a Report from a Query	212
4	Exporting Information	218
5	Importing Information	222
6	Appending Data from One Table to Another	226
7	Using Name AutoCorrect	230
8	Viewing Data with Subdatasheets	234
9	Creating Subdatasheets	236
10	Creating a Data Access Page	238
11	Working with Data on a Page	242
12	Editing the Data Access Page Design	244

Permanent relationships are created between tables that each have a field whose data type is compatible with the other, and where the data from one table can be matched to the information contained in the second. This can provide an automatic link when you build forms, queries, and reports.

A permanent relationship also enables you to set up referential integrity between fields. For example, a permanent relation between an orders table and a customer table with referential integrity would not allow you to place an order if the customer does not yet exist.

Task 1: Building Permanent Relationships

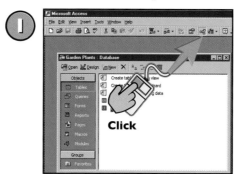

Click

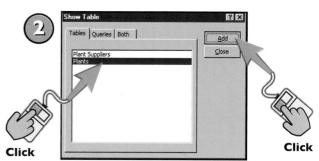

Click

Click

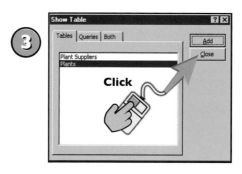

Click

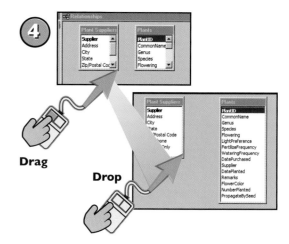

Drag

Drop

① Open the **Garden Plants** database and click the Relationships button on the toolbar.

② Select both the **Plant Suppliers** and **Plants** tables from the list and click the **Add** button, placing each on the Relationships window.

③ Click the **Close** button when you're finished.

④ Increase the size of the list boxes so that you can easily see all the fields.

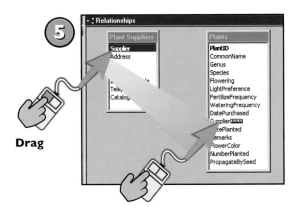

Drag

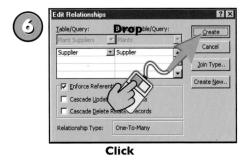

Click

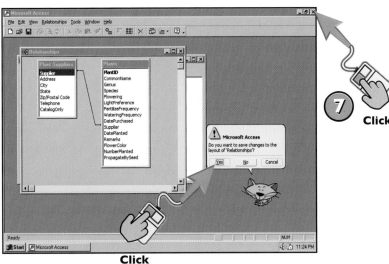

Click

Click

✓ **Related Fields**
You should always drag the primary key field and drop it onto the foreign key field.

✓ **Adding to the Relationships**
You can add new tables to the relationship layout at any time, or delete existing relationships.

5️⃣ Click the **Supplier** field in the **Plant Suppliers** list and drag it onto the **Supplier** field in the **Plants** list.

6️⃣ The Edit Relationships dialog box opens. Click the **Create** button. A dialog box is displayed with more information if any problems occur.

7️⃣ Close the Relationships window by clicking the Close (**X**) button.

8️⃣ When prompted by the Office Assistant, save the layout.

End Task

The most efficient way to work with information in two or more tables is to use a query. Through the query, and forms and reports based on the query, you can view, edit, or add information into any tables on which the query is based. You can use a query to funnel information from many sources, through one point, and then into the appropriate tables.

In this task, you will create a query that will display those records that are linked together in both the Plants and Plant Suppliers tables.

Task 2: Using a Query with Multiple Tables

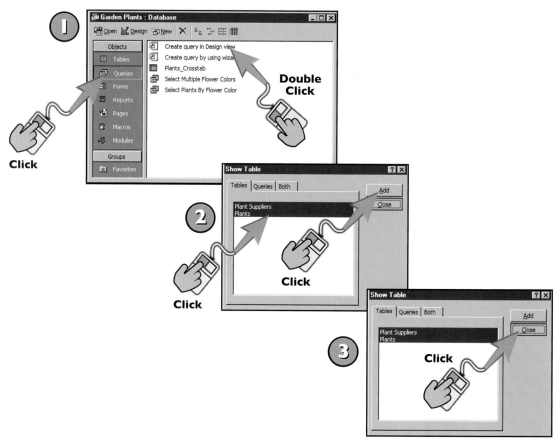

(1) Click the **Queries** object button, then double-click **Create query in Design view**.

(2) Select both **Plant Suppliers** and **Plants** from the list, and click **Add** to place them on the query window.

(3) Click the **Close** button.

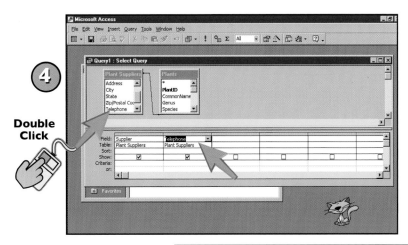

Double Click

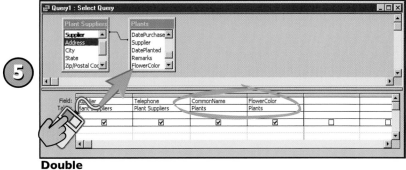

Double Click

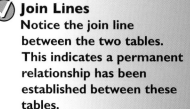

4 From the Plant Suppliers list add the fields **Supplier** and **Telephone** to the query grid by double-clicking each.

5 From the **Plants** table list, add **CommonName** and **FlowerColor** to the query grid by double-clicking them.

✓ **Join Lines**
Notice the join line between the two tables. This indicates a permanent relationship has been established between these tables.

Next Step

Using a Query with Multiple Tables Continued

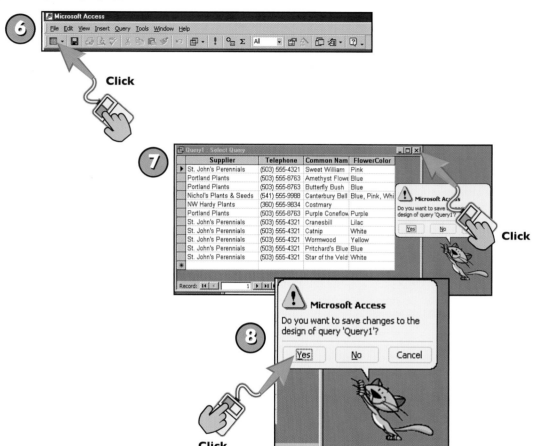

Click

No Records Displayed?
If no records are displayed, be sure that the supplier name in the Plant Suppliers table exactly matches the entry in the Suppliers field in the Plants table. Access is looking for matching values in both tables.

 Click the View button to see the resulting datasheet.

 Click the Close (**X**) button.

 Click the **Yes** button when prompted to save the query.

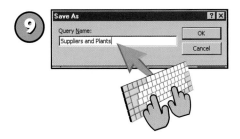

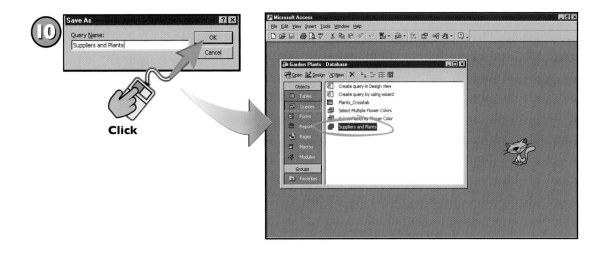

Type **Suppliers and Plants** in the text box of the Save As dialog box.

Click **OK** to save the query. You will see the new query has been added to the Queries list.

PART

Task 3: Creating a Report from a Query

Often, reports are based on a query instead of on a table. This enables you to do two things: select the records that meet the report requirements, and combine information from multiple tables. By using a query, you can select records by customer, by time period, by product, or by other criteria. This can help you focus your report on the information you need to present, instead of making it so general that the information is overwhelmingly detailed. This also ensures that your report has the latest data. This task shows you how to use a query to combine the information from two tables, and then base a report on it.

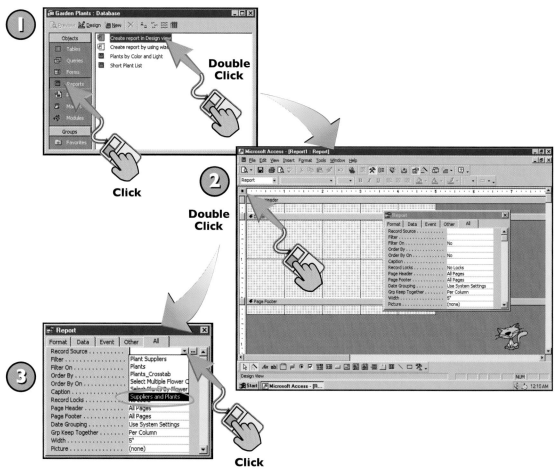

① Select the **Reports** object, then double-click the **Create report in Design view** option. Be sure to maximize the window to give yourself working room.

② Double-click the Report Selector button in the upper-left corner of the window to display its property sheet.

③ Click the down-arrow button in the **Record Source** property and select the **Suppliers and Plants** query as the basis for the report.

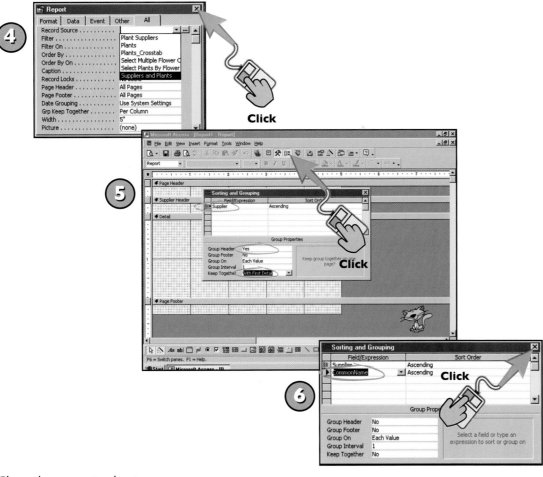

Click

Click

Click

(4) Close the property sheet.

(5) Click the Sorting and Grouping button on the toolbar. Select **Supplier** on the first row, then select **Yes** for Group Header and **With First Detail** in Keep Together.

(6) Move the cursor to the second row beneath **Supplier**, and select **CommonName**. The default sort order of Ascending is what you want. Close this dialog box.

Creating a Report from a Query Continued

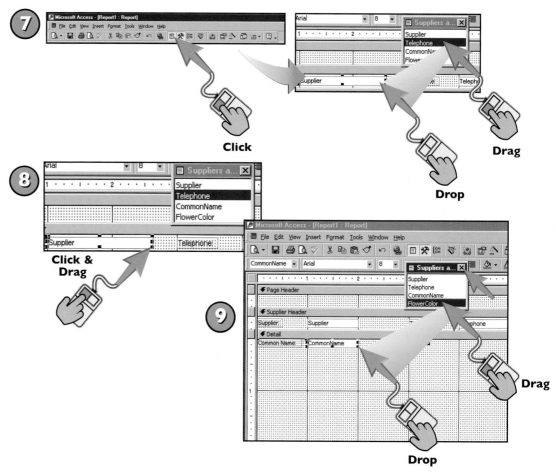

Click

Drag

Drop

Click & Drag

Drag

Drop

⑦ Click the Field List button, and drag both the **Supplier** and **Telephone** fields to the Supplier Header grid.

⑧ Increase the length of the **Suppliers** field by dragging the right edge.

⑨ Select both **CommonName** and **FlowerColor** and drag them to the Detail grid. Close the Field List.

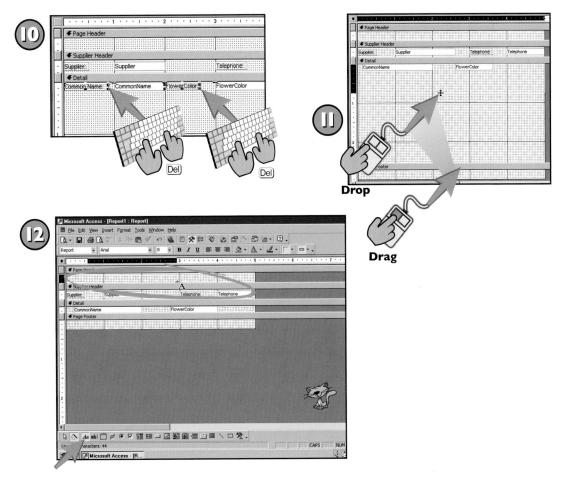

Drop

Drag

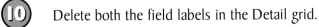

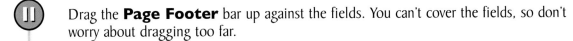

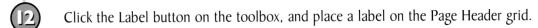

Delete both the field labels in the Detail grid.

Drag the **Page Footer** bar up against the fields. You can't cover the fields, so don't worry about dragging too far.

Click the Label button on the toolbox, and place a label on the Page Header grid.

Creating a Report from a Query Continued

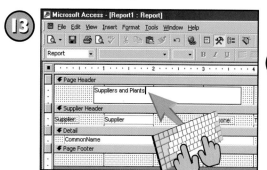

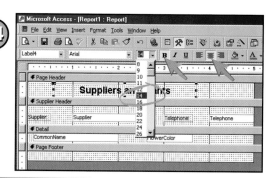

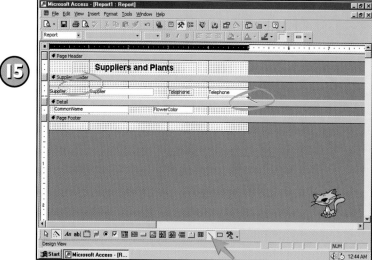

13 Type **Suppliers and Plants**, and press Enter.

14 Click the Bold and Center buttons, and increase the font size from 8 to **14**.

15 Click the Line button on the toolbox and draw two lines, one above and one below the Supplier and Telephone fields in the Supplier header grid.

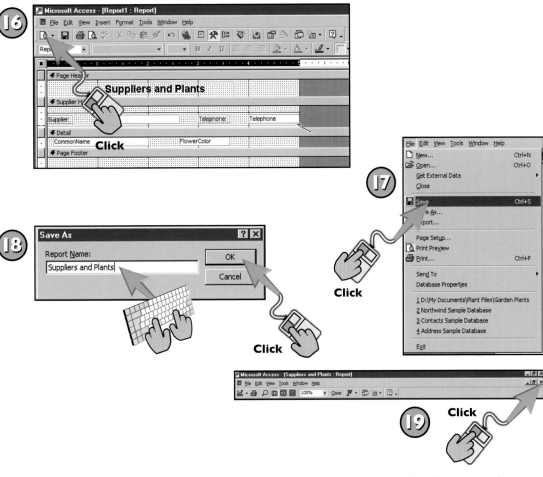

(16) Click the View button. Be sure to check the sort order of your groups, the alignment of detail records and labels, and the page layout.

(17) Click **File**, **Save** from the menu.

(18) In the Save As dialog box type **Suppliers and Plants** in the text box and click **OK**.

(19) Click the Close (**X**) button.

Task 4: Exporting Information

You can share information with other applications by exporting selected tables. When you export information from Access, you can choose from several file formats. When you export information, you must know what application the information will be imported into: another Access database or a different database program, or will the data be used in a word processor or spreadsheet? You have many choices, but when in doubt, you can always export as a text file. Most applications can import a text file.

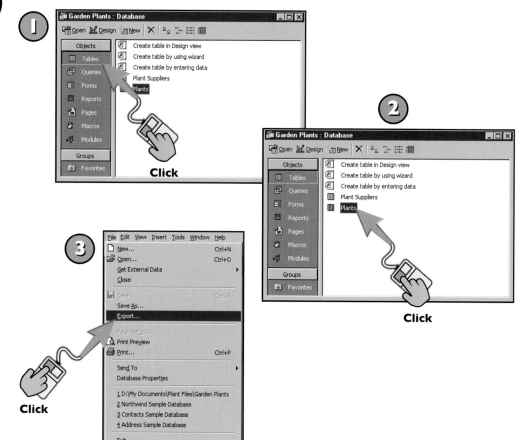

1. Click the **Tables** object button.

2. Click the **Plants** table.

3. Click **File**, **Export** from the menu, opening the Export Table To dialog box.

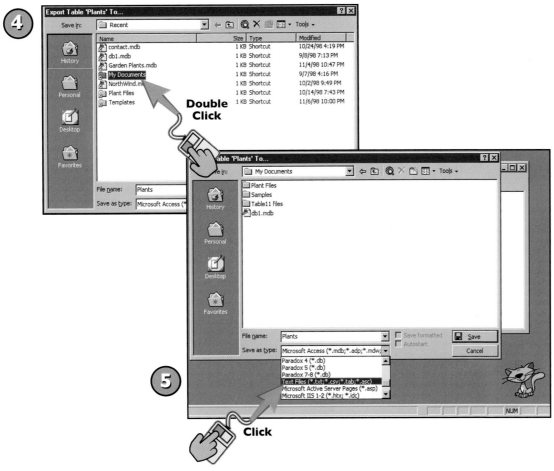

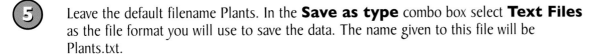

④ Double-click the **My Documents** shortcut to open that folder.

⑤ Leave the default filename Plants. In the **Save as type** combo box select **Text Files** as the file format you will use to save the data. The name given to this file will be Plants.txt.

Exporting Information Continued

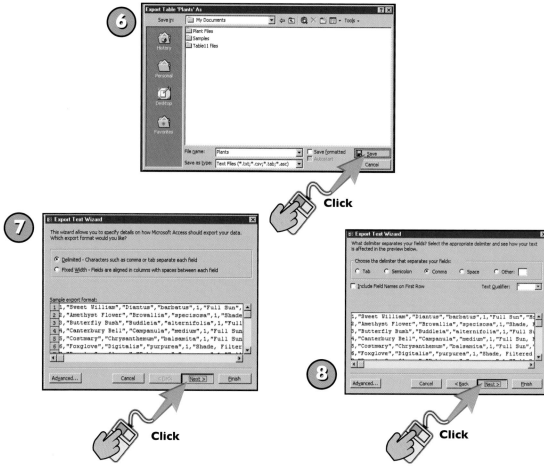

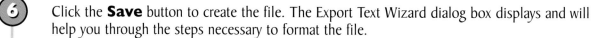

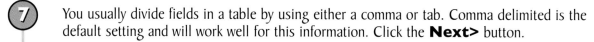

6 Click the **Save** button to create the file. The Export Text Wizard dialog box displays and will help you through the steps necessary to format the file.

7 You usually divide fields in a table by using either a comma or tab. Comma delimited is the default setting and will work well for this information. Click the **Next>** button.

8 Use the default options for this file. If you want to include the field names as the first row, then you would check that box. Click the **Next>** button.

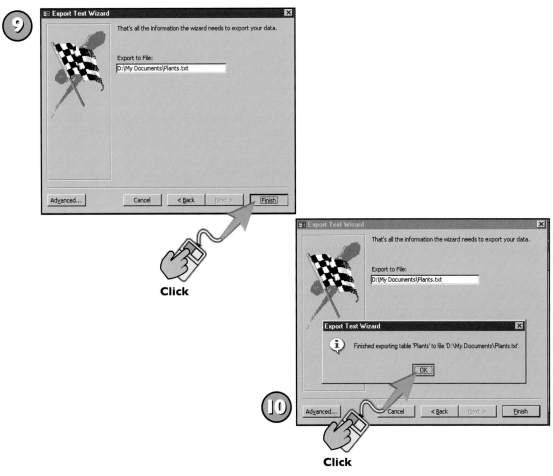

Click

Click

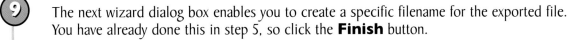

The next wizard dialog box enables you to create a specific filename for the exported file. You have already done this in step 5, so click the **Finish** button.

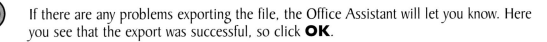

If there are any problems exporting the file, the Office Assistant will let you know. Here you see that the export was successful, so click **OK**.

Task 5: Importing Information

Access can also import information from a variety of other applications. You can import data from another database, a spreadsheet, or from a text file. In this task you will import the text file that you just created.

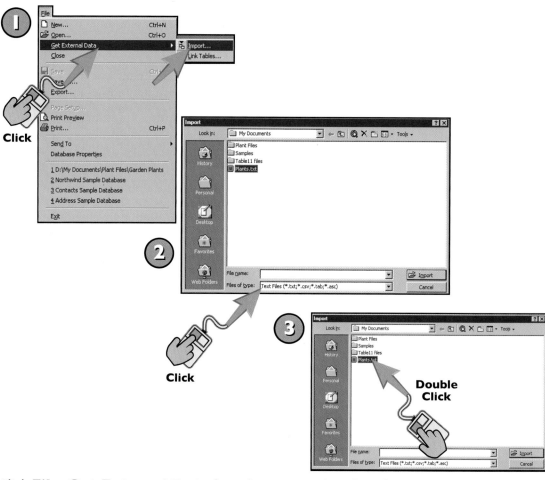

① Click **File**, **Get External Data** from the menu, and on the submenu select **Import**.

② The Import dialog box opens. Select **Text Files** from the **Files of type** combo box.

③ You will now see the **Plants** file displayed in the list box. Double-click **Plants.txt**.

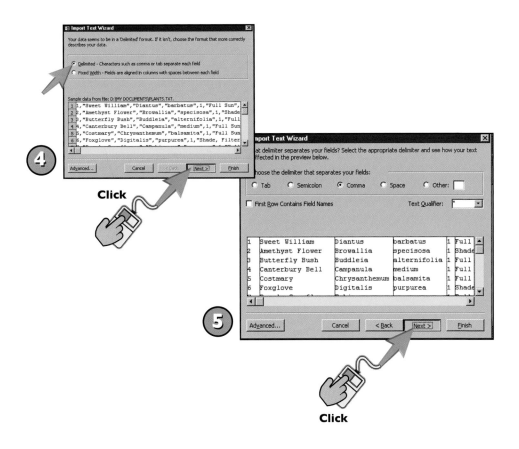

Click

Click

④ The Import Text Wizard dialog box opens. Plants.txt is a delimited file. Be sure the **Delimited** option button is selected, and then click the **Next>** button.

⑤ The fields are all lined up and divided at the proper places. If they aren't, then choose another delimiter option button until they are lined up. Click the **Next>** button.

✓ **Finding the Delimiter**
If you can't determine the character used as a delimiter, open the file in Word and see what character is displayed between each field. Use that character in the Other text box.

Importing Information Continued

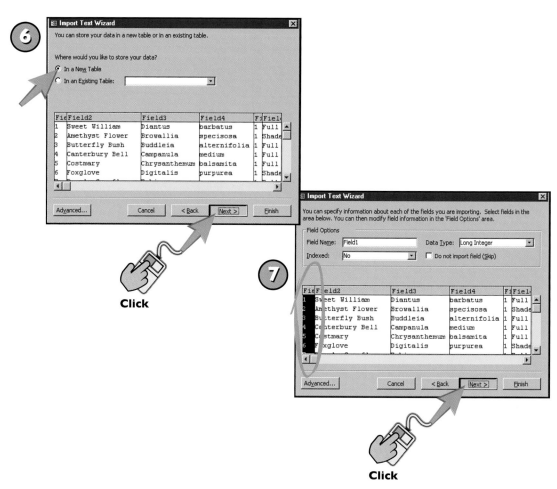

Click

Click

 Importing to an Existing Table

When importing into an existing table, the imported data must have the same number of fields and same data types as the table. You can't import into a field that uses the AutoNumber data type.

6 You can store the imported data in a new table that the wizard creates or in an existing table. Select the **In a New Table** option button, and then click the **Next>** button.

7 In this dialog box you tell Access about the data you are importing. You can choose to not import fields by skipping them, and select data types for fields. Click the **Next>** button.

 Next Step

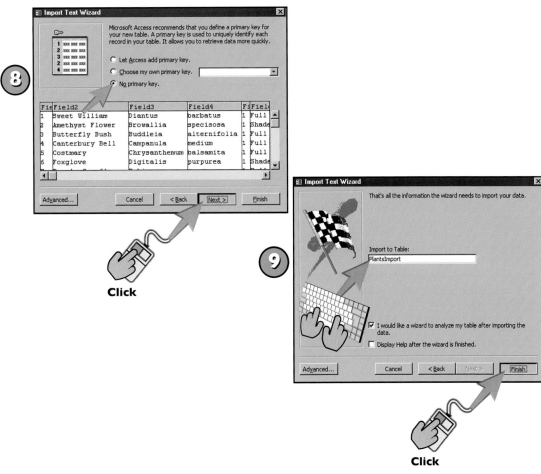

Click

Click

⑧ Select the **No Primary Key** option button and click the **Next>** button.

⑨ Type **PlantsImport** as the table name, and then click the **Finish** button.

Task 6: Appending Data from One Table to Another

Start Here

You can use a query to append records from one table to another. This is commonly done when you have imported data from one file into a temporary holding table as you did in Task 5. This gives you the option to check the information and do any necessary cleanup before appending the information into a live table.

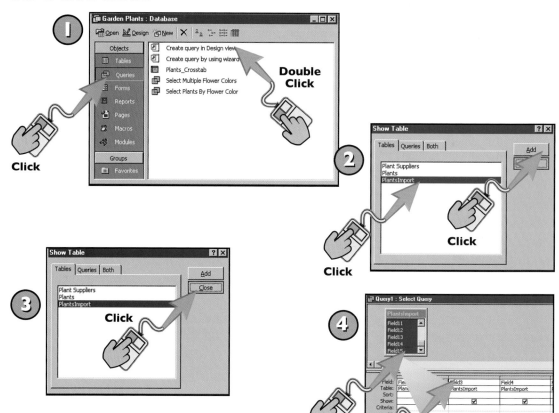

(1) Click the **Queries** object button, and double-click the **Create query in Design view** option.

(2) Select the **PlantsImport** table and add it.

(3) Click the **Close** button.

(4) Add all the fields to the query grid, except Field1. You can select multiple fields in the list, and then drag them to the grid in one step. Ignore the asterisk option.

Next Step

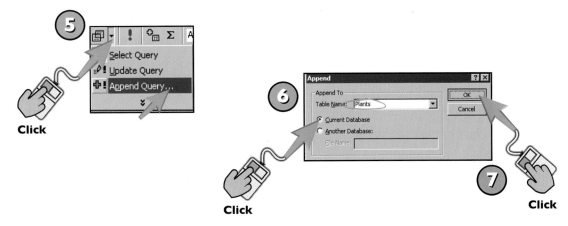

Click

Click

Click

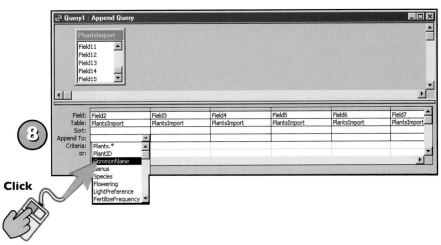

Click

5   Click the down-arrow button part of the Query Type button and select **Append Query** from the list.

6   The Append dialog box appears. Select **Plants** in the **Table Name** combo box, and the **Current Database** option button.

7   Click **OK**. The **Append To** row is added to the query and used to map data from the PlantsImport table to a field in the Plants table.

8   In the **Field2** column select **CommonName** from the **Append To** combo box.

Next Step

Appending Data from One Table to Another Continued

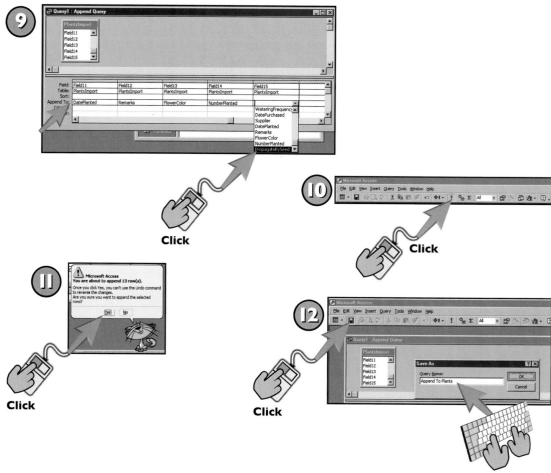

Click

Click

Click

Click

9 Continue with each of the remaining columns: Field3 = Genus, Field4 = Species, and so on for each remaining field.

10 Start the query by clicking the Run button.

11 Click the **Yes** button to append the new records. Clicking **No** cancels the procedure.

12 Click the Save button, and name the query **Append To Plants**.

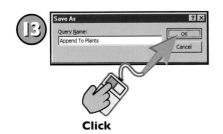

Click

Click

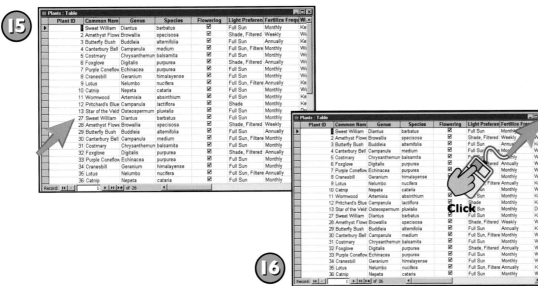

Click

(13) Click **OK**.

(14) Click Close (**X**) to close the query.

(15) Open the Plants table. See the new records that have been added. All records after PlantID 13 are appended records. Your own table might have numbered these 14 on up.

(16) Close the Plants table.

✓ Why Are There Missing Numbers?
When you use an AutoNumber data type, records are numbered sequentially. If you delete a record, its number is never reused. If you have records 1–10 and delete 8 and 9, you have records 1–7 and 10. If you add two records, they will be 11 and 12, not 8 and 9.

Name AutoCorrect is a new feature of Access 2000 that is turned on by default. In earlier versions, if you change the name of a field in a table, any queries, forms, and reports will lose their connections to that field. You must manually correct each object. Name AutoCorrect automatically updates all the objects that reference the field name that you change.

Task 7: Using Name AutoCorrect

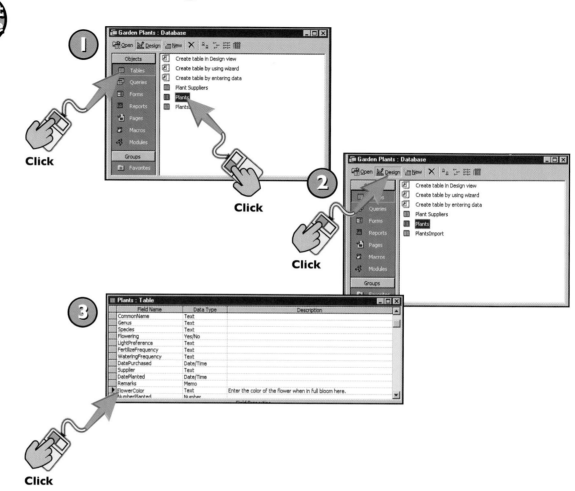

Click

Click

Click

Click

1 Click the **Tables** object button, and then click the **Plants** table.

2 Click the **Design** button to open the Plants table in Design view.

3 Click **FlowerColor** in the Field Name column, and delete the word **Flower**.

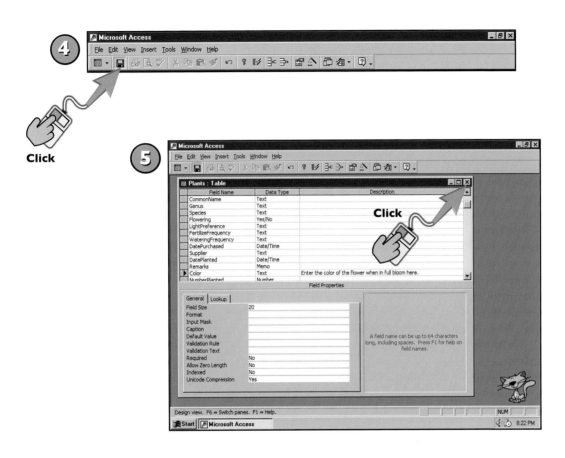

Click

Click

④ Click the Save button.

⑤ Click the Close (**X**) button.

Using Name AutoCorrect Continued

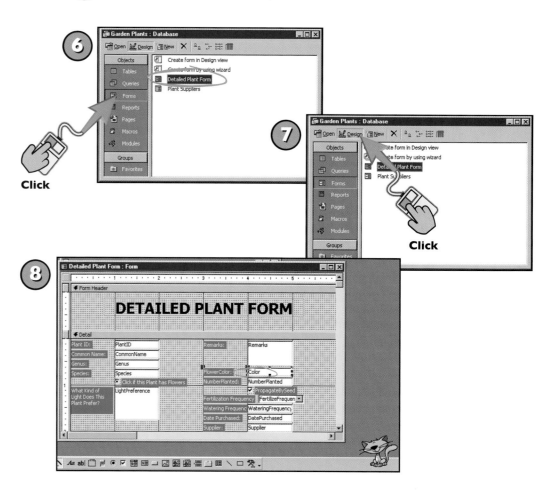

Click

Click

(6) Click the **Forms** object button, and then select **Detailed Plant Form**.

(7) Click the **Design** button.

(8) Notice the **Color** field. This was the FlowerColor field; Name AutoCorrect has updated the name.

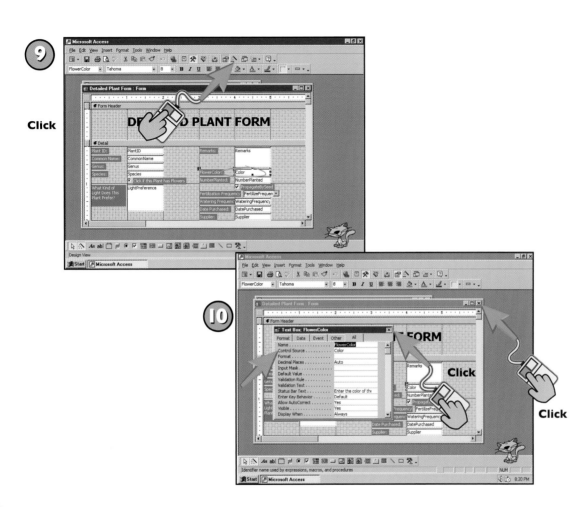

Click

Click

Click

 Select the **Color** field, and then click the Properties button to display the property sheet.

 The Control Source is now **Color**. Close the property sheet and the form.

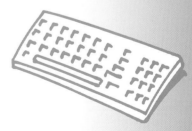

Task 8: Viewing Data with Subdatasheets

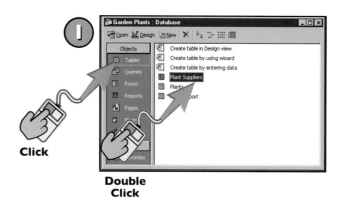

Click

Double Click

Subdatasheets are new to Access 2000. When a relationship exists between tables or queries, a subdatasheet that shows all the related records can be displayed. Subdatasheets can display information from a related table or the datasheet from a query. If a relationship has not already been set, Access can create it for you, adding it to the Relationship diagram. You can have only one subdatasheet per table or query, but they can be nested up to eight deep. Access added a special column in the Suppliers table when you created a relationship in Task 1 of this part.

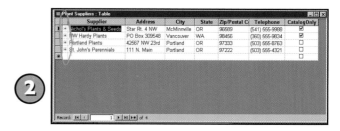

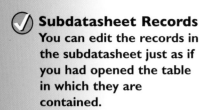

✓ **Subdatasheet Records**
You can edit the records in the subdatasheet just as if you had opened the table in which they are contained.

Click the **Tables** objects button, and then double-click the **Plant Suppliers** table to open it.

The Plant Suppliers table is opened. See the new column to the left of the records with a plus sign (+) beside each record. This shows that a subdatasheet is available.

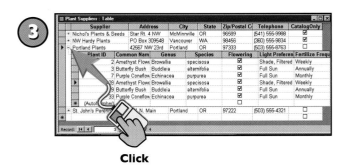

Click

Click

③ Click the **+** beside **Portland Plants**, making it a minus sign and displaying the subdatasheet showing all plants purchased from this company.

④ Close the table by clicking the Close (**X**) button.

Task 9: Creating Subdatasheets

Subdatasheets can be added to tables or queries even if a permanent relationship has not been created. To add a subdatasheet, each object must have a field that can be used to create a relationship with.

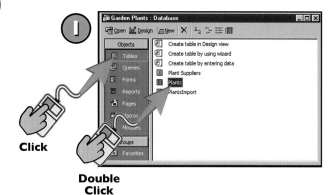

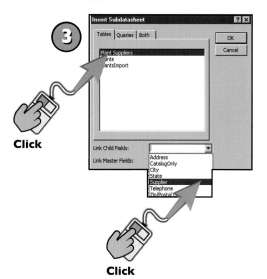

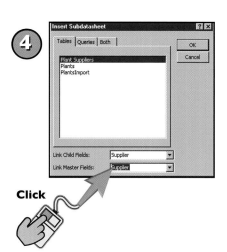

 Click the **Tables** objects button, and then double-click the **Plants** table to open it.

 Click **Insert**, **Subdatasheet** from the menu to open the Insert Subdatasheet dialog box.

 Click **Plant Suppliers** in the **Tables** list. Click the **Link Child Fields** combo box and select **Supplier**.

 In the **Link Master Fields** box select **Supplier**. This field creates a link from the Plant Suppliers table to the Plants table; you create a one in the other direction.

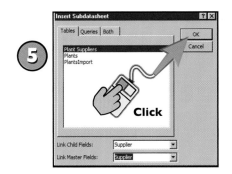

5

Click

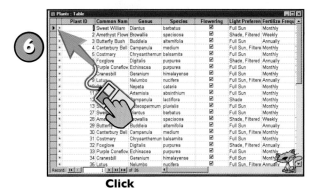

6

Click

7

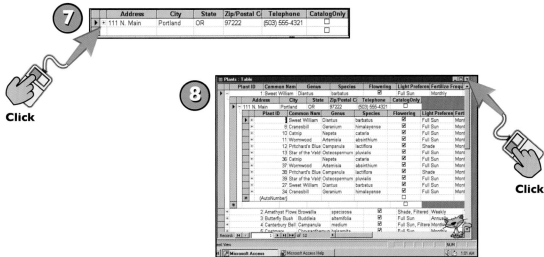

Click

8

Click

5 Click **OK**. Access inserts the subdatasheet column in the Plants table.

6 Click the **+** button beside the record for Sweet William. The subdatasheet opens, displaying the data for the supplier of this plant.

7 Click the **+** sign beside the supplier address.

8 Another subdatasheet opens, showing all the plants sold to you by this supplier. These are nested subdatasheets. Close the table by clicking its Close (**X**) button.

End Task

Where's the Name?
The name or other link field is not displayed in a subdatasheet. You can unhide the column by selecting **Format, Unhide Columns** from the menu.

Task 10: Creating a Data Access Page

You can create a data access page by using a wizard or a Design view type window. The simplest method is the wizard, but this method does not give you the same degree of control you would get when building the page from scratch. Creating a data access page is similar to the processes you have learned to build forms and reports. Many of the same objects and tools you have already worked with are used to create a data access page. You can build a data access page so that the information contained in it can be edited and returned to the Access table, and you can update it with the new information. You can also create pages that let someone view information without being able to make changes. Data access pages are contained within a file that is separate from Access 2000 or any of its databases.

Start Here

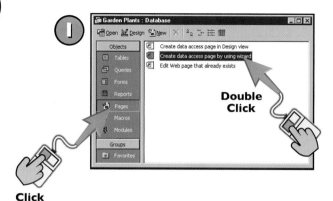
Double Click

Click

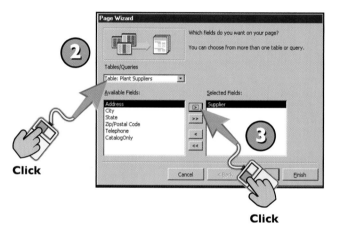
Click

Click

1. Click the **Pages** object button, then double-click the **Create data access page by using wizard** option.

2. Select **Table: Plant Suppliers** in the **Tables/Queries** combo box.

3. Click the **>** button to move the Supplier field to the **Selected Fields** list box.

Next Step

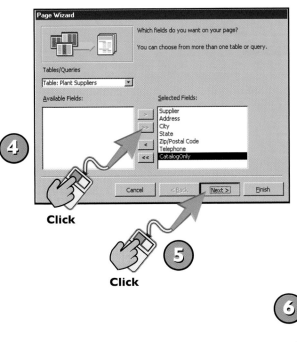

Click

Click

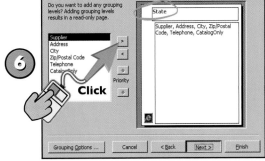

Click

4. Click the **>>** button to select and move the remaining fields to the **Selected Fields** list box.

5. Click the **Next>** button to continue.

6. Group the records by selecting the **State** field and clicking the **>** button.

✓ **Prerequisites**
In order for someone to view and use a data access page, they must have a copy of Internet Explorer 5 or later and a Microsoft Office 2000 license. They do not have to have Office loaded on their computer.

Creating a Data Access Page Continued

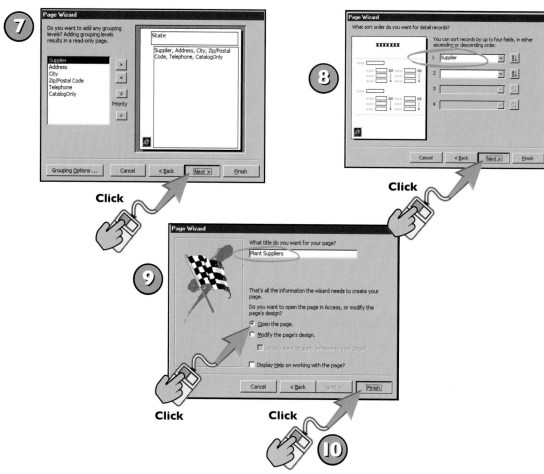

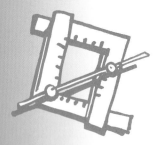

⑦ Click the **Next>** button.

⑧ Select **Supplier** in the first combo box as the field to use for sorting the detail records within each State group. Click the **Next>** button.

⑨ Type a title for the page or accept the default—which you will do here. Select the option button **Open the page**.

⑩ Click the **Finish** button.

Next
Step

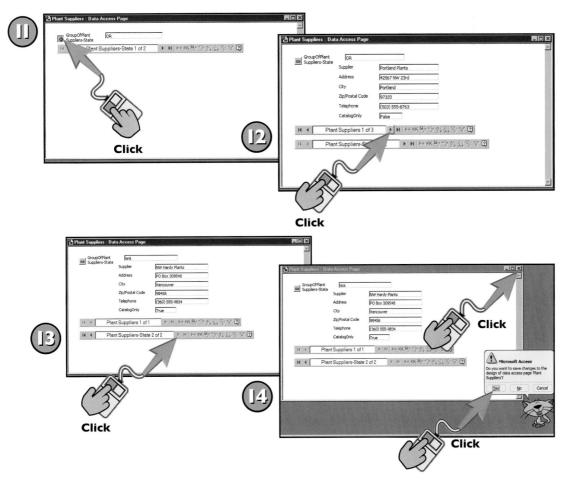

Click

Click

Click

Click

The new data access page opens in its own window. Click the **+** button to see the first detail record of the group.

Click the right-arrow record navigation button beside **Plant Suppliers 1 of 3** to view the next record.

Click the right-arrow record navigation on the lower bar to view the next group. Expand the group by clicking the **+** button.

Click the Close (**X**) button when finished, and click **Yes** when prompted by the Office Assistant to save the data access page.

Task 11: Working with Data on a Page

Depending on the type of data access page you are using, and possibly your access permissions, you can use a page to view, add, or update records in an Access table. Some pages are created so that you can view current information, but you are not allowed to change or add data. Others can give you permission to work with the data as if you were working in the actual Access table. In the previous task, you saw how records could be viewed in a page.

Start Here

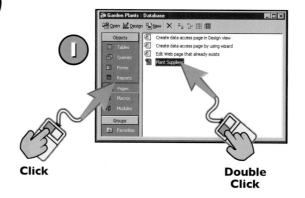

Click

Double Click

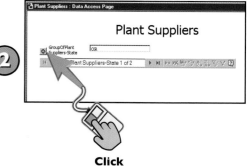

Click

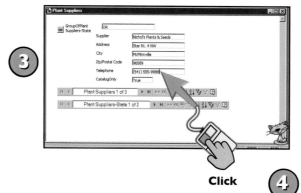

Click

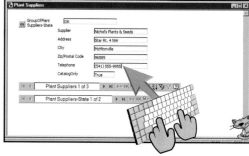

Click

 Click the **Pages** object button, and then double-click the **Plant Suppliers** page object, opening it.

 Click the **+** button to expand the detail records. This company has changed its telephone number.

 Click in the Telephone field box.

 Press the Backspace key twice, deleting the 88. Type **55**, which is the new number.

Next Step

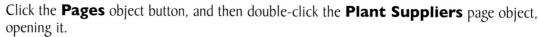

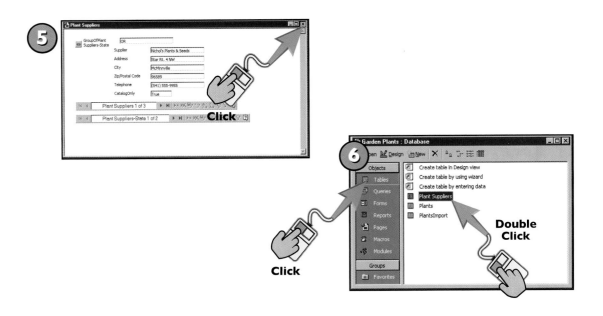

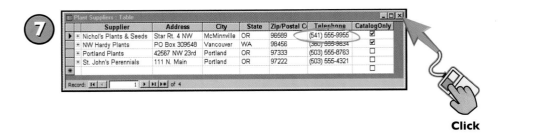

5 Click the Close (**X**) button.

6 Click the **Tables** object button and double-click the **Plant Suppliers** table.

7 You can see that the telephone number has been updated for the first supplier. Close the table.

Task 12: Editing the Data Access Page Design

As with other Access objects such as forms and reports, you can change the design of a data access page. The process is similar to working in the Design view window for a form or report, but there are some differences. Some of the tools on the toolbox toolbar are different, as are some of the other properties that you have become used to, such as being able to add themes to your pages and include other Web-like objects.

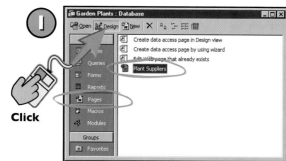

Click

Click

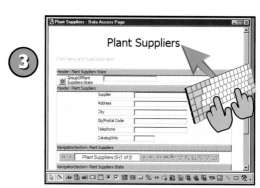

① Select the **Pages** object button and the **Plant Suppliers** data access page. Click the **Design** button.

② Click on the text that says **Click here and type title text**. This text will disappear.

③ Type **Plant Suppliers** as the new title for this page. The body text area can be used to include other needed information about the page.

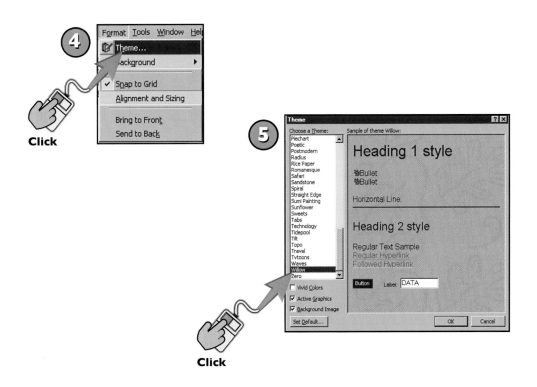

4 Click **Format, Theme** from the menu to open the Theme dialog box. You can select a wide variety of themes for your data access pages.

5 Scroll down the **Choose a Theme** list box and select **Willow** as the theme for this page. A sample is displayed in the box beside the name.

Editing the Data Access Page Design Continued

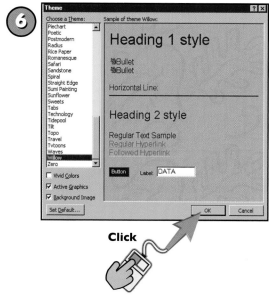

Click

Click 8

7

Click

6 Click **OK** to apply the theme.

7 Click the Save button.

8 Click the View button to see how the page looks.

Click

Click

⑨ Click the Close (**X**) button to return to the Database window.

⑩ Be sure to click **Yes** when prompted by the Office Assistant to save the changes you have made.

Appendix A

Tables

In Part 3, Task 1, "Entering New Information in a Table," you will need to enter the information contained in Tables 3.1 and 3.2. The tables contain the information needed for the records that you will use throughout the rest of this book. Be sure to enter the information exactly as shown, including see last table for other instructions typos. Table 3.3 contains the information you need for Part 3, Task 2, "Completing the Supplier Table."

Table 3.1

Common Name	Genus	Species	Flowering	Light Preference	Fertilize Frequency	Watering Frequency
Amethyst Flower	Browallia	speciosa	Yes ✓	Shade,Filtered Sun	Weekly	Weekly
Butterfly Bbush	buddleia	alternifolia	Yes ✓	Full Sun	Annually	Keep Dry
Canterbury Bell	Campanula	medium	Yes ✓	Full Sun,Filtered Sun	Monthly	Weekly
Costmary	Chrysanthemum	balsamita	Yes ✓	Full Sun	Monthly	Weekly
Foxglove	Digitalis	purpurea	Yes ✓	Shade,Filtered Sun	Annually	Weekly
Purple Coneflower	Echinacea	purpurea	Yes ✓	Full Sun	Monthly	Weekly
Cranesbill	Geranium	himalayense	Yes ✓	Full Sun	Monthly	Weekly
Lotus	Nelumbo	nucifera	Yes ✓	Full Sun,Filtered Sun	Annually	Keep Wet
catnip	Nepeta	cataria	Yes ✓	Full Sun	Monthly	Weekly
Wormwood	Artemisia	absinthium	Yes ✓	Full Sun	Monthly	Keep Dry

Table 3.2

Common Name	Date Purchased	Place Purchased	Date Planted	Remarks	Flower Color	Number Planted	Propagate by Seed
Amethyst Flower	3/1/98	Portland Plants	3/2/98	Annual, may be perennial	Blue	6	Yes ☑
Butterfly Bbush	5/15/95	Portland Plants	5/20/95	Perennial	Blue	2	Yes ☑
Canterbury Bell	12/10/96	Nichol's Plants & Seeds	2/1/96	Biennial	Blue, Pink, White	15	Yes ☑
Costmary	3/15/97	NW Hardy Plants	3/15/97	Perennial		3	No
Foxglove	5/1/94	N/A	6/1/94	Biennial, perennial	Purple	12	Yes ☑
Purple Coneflower	3/1/96	Portland Plants	3/2/96	Perennial	Purple	3	Yes ☑
Cranesbill	6/1/97	St. John's Perennials	6/1/97	Perennial	Lilac	2	Yes ☑
Lotus	3/15/97	Portland Pond's	3/15/97	Perennial	Pink	2	No
catnip	6/1/95	St. John's Perennials	6/3/95	Perennial	White	6	Yes ☑
Wormwood	4/15/96	St. John's Perennials	4/20/96	Perennial	Yellow	1	Yes ☑

Table 3.3

Supplier	Address	City	State	Zip/Postal Code	Telephone	Catalog Only
St. John's Perennials	111 N. Main	Portland	OR	97222	(503)555-4231	(empty)
Portland Plants	42567 NW 23rd	Portland	OR	97333	(503)555-8763	(empty)
NW Hardy Check Plants	PO Box 309548	Vancouver	WA	98456	(360)555-9834	(empty)
Nichol's Plants & Seeds	Star Rt. 4 NW	McMinnville	OR	96589	(541)555-9988	Check

Symbols

* (asterisk) wildcard, 152
? (question mark) wildcard, 152

A

Access 2000
   exiting, 33
   installing, 4-6
   Internet site, help, 32
   starting, 8-9, 36
accessing help, 20
action queries, 140
   deleting records, 162
Add button, 142
adding
   date and time automatically, 180
   effects, reports, 196-199
   fields
      calculated, 124-127
      in Datasheet view, 58
      in Design view, 44
      queries, 160
      to reports, 177
   fields to forms, 104-105
   folders for databases, 36-37
   number fields, 46-47
   page numbers automatically, 180
   pop-up tips, 128-129
adding fields to the query grid,
   148-151, 160
Answer Wizard, 20
   searching help, 24-25
Answer Wizard tab button, 24
Append dialog box, 227
appending data between tables,
   226-229
Apply Filter button, 85
arithmatic operators, queries, 158
asking questions with Office Assistant,
   30-31

asterisks, 152
AutoForm, 96
AutoNumber data types, 66
Available Fields list, 99

B

Back button, 22
bars
   Detail, 110
   Form Footer, 124
   Page Footer, 215
Blank Access Database option button,
   36
Bold button, 111, 179
Box tool, 199
boxes
   combo, 112-115
   Control Source, 126
   list, 116-117
build button, 126, 193
building relationships, permanent,
   206-207
buttons
   Add, 142
   Answer Wizard tab, 24
   Apply Filter, 85
   Back, 22
   Blank Database option, 36
   Bold, 111, 179
   Build, 193
   building, 126
   Cancel, 81
   Center, 111, 179
   Close, 97, 143-146
   Combo Box, 112
   Contents tab (help), 21
   Control Wizards, 112
   Create, 39, 207
   Create New Folder, 37
   Customize, 5
   Cut, 181
   Delimited, 223
   Design, 56, 166
   Desktop, 10, 37

down-arrow, 130
Field List, 177, 214
Fill/Back Color, 199
Filter by Form, 84
Filter By Selection, 83
Find, 76
Find Next, 77-81
Finish, 101, 115, 174
Font Size, 178
Forms, 232
Forms object, 98, 133
Forward, 22
In a New Table, 224
Index tab (Help window), 26
Install Now, 7
Label, 110, 178, 192, 215
Large Icons, 16
light bulb, 20
List Box, 116
List toolbar, 16
Modify the table design button, 43
More, 77
New, 98, 176
New Object, 96
New Record, 134
Next, 5, 42, 100
No, 55, 97
No Primary Key, 225
object
   choosing, 17
   Forms, 17
OK, 37, 132
Open, 13, 51
Open the page, 240
option, 122-123
Pages, 242
Paste, 181
Personal, 40
Primary Key, 62
Print, 203
Properties, 125
Queries, 142, 208, 226
Queries tab, 148
Query Type, 164, 227
Relationships, 206
Remove Filter, 83-85

Replace, 81
Replace All, 81
Report, 170
Report Selector, 212
Run, 228
Save, 132, 202
Show, 20
Sort Ascending, 82
Sorting and Grouping, 182-184
Start, 8, 36
Tables, 40, 60, 218, 230
Text Box, 124, 193
toolbars, 16
Undo, 74
View, 57, 129, 200
Yes, 146, 210

C

calculated fields
    adding, 124, 127
    queries, 161
    reports, 192-195
Cancel button, 81
Center button, 111, 179
changing
    color in forms, 130-131
    field
        names, 52-53
        order, 136-137
Check Box control, 107
check boxes
    Match Case (Find and Replace dialog
        box), 78
    Show, 161
choosing
    object buttons, 17
    Office Assistant, 28-29
Close button, 97, 143-146
colors (forms), changing, 130-131
columns
    freezing, 90
    hiding, 92-93

resizing, 88-89
unfreezing, 90
unhiding, 92
Combo Box button, 112
Combo Box Wizard dialog box, 113
combo boxes, 112-115
commands
    dialog boxes, 14
    Edit menu, Replace, 80
    File menu
        Exit, 33
        Export, 218
        Import, 222
        Page Setup, 200
        Print, 203
    Format menu
        Freeze Columns, 90
        Hide Columns, 92
        Theme, 245
        Unhide Columns, 93
    Help menu, What's This, 23
    Insert menu
        Date and Time, 180
        Page Numbers, 180
        Subdatasheet, 236
    menu, 14-15
    View menu
        Database Objects, 15
        Form Header/Footer, 108
        Report Header/Footer, 178
Contents help, 20
Contents tab button (help), 21
context-sensitive help, 23
Control Source box, 126
Control Source text box, 122
Control Wizards button, 112
controls
    Check Box, 107
    combo boxes, 112-115
    list boxes, 116-117
    option buttons, 122-123
ControlTip Text property, 128
copying
    records, 70-71
    shortcuts, 71

Create button, 39, 207
Create New Folder button, 37
Create query in Design view option,
    142
creating
    AutoForms, 96
    data access page, 238-241
    databases, 38-39
    labels, 110
    reports
        queries, 212-217
        with Report Wizard, 170-175
    subdatasheets, 236-237
    tables
        from scratch, 60-62
        with Table Wizard, 40-43
criteria (queries), 140
    changing, 166
    multiple criterion, 156
    OR, 154-155
crosstab queries, 140
    creating, 148-151
Crosstab Query Wizard, 148
Customize button, 5
customizing Office Assistant, 29
Cut button, 181

D

data
    editing, 64
        fields, 72
    entering, 64
    pages, 242-243
    subdatasheets, viewing, 234-235
    tables, appending, 226-229
data access page
    creating, 238-241
    editing, 242-244
Data Type column (fields), 44
data types, AutoNumber, 66
database forms
    AutoForms, 96
    color, changing, 130-131

database forms

combo boxes, 112
creating with Form Wizard, 98-99
fields
    adding, 99, 104-105
    calculated, 124-127
    changing order, 136-137
    moving in Form Design view,
        106-107
    pop-up tip text, adding, 128-129
Form Design View window, 102
headers and footers, 108
implementing, 94
information, editing, 134-135
labels
    creating, 110
    editing, 120-121
list boxes, 116-117
objects, moving, 118
opening, 133
option buttons, 122-123
saving, 132
tasks
    saving, 132
    Using a Combo Box, 115

**Database Objects command
(View menu), 15**

databases
    creating, 38-39
    fields, editing, 72
    filtering by form, 83-84
    folders, adding, 36-37
    opening, 10-13
    records
        copying, 70-71
        deleting, 86
        sorting, 82
    replacing selected information, 80-81
    retrieving information. See queries
    searching, 76-79
    tables
        entering new information, 66-69
        freezing and unfreezing, 90
        hiding and unhiding columns, 92
        resizing rows and columns, 88-89
Datasheet view, fields, adding, 58
**date and time, adding automatically,
180**

**Date and Time command (Insert
menu), 180**
Date and Time dialog box, 180
Definitions (tables), saving, 50
deleting
    fields, 59
    records, 86
        with queries, 162
    text, 73
Delimited button, 223
Description column (fields), 45
deselecting fields, 99
Design button, 56, 166
Design view
    fields, adding, 44
    reports, opening, 176
    window, 60
Desktop button, 10, 37
Detail area, forms, 104
Detail bar, 110
dialog balloon, Office Assistant, 30
dialog boxes
    Append, 227
    Combo Box Wizard, 113
    commands, 14
    Crosstab Query Wizard, 148
    Date and Time, 180
    Edit Relationships, 207
    Export Table To, 218
    Export Text Wizard, 220
    Expression Builder, 126, 195
    File New Database, 36
    Find and Replace, 76
    Import Text Wizard, 223
    New Form, 98
    New Query, 148
    New Table, 60
    Office Assistant, 29
    Page Numbers, 180
    Page Setup, 200
    Print, 203
    Save As, 132, 147
    Show Table, 142, 152
    Sorting and Grouping, 182
down-arrow button, 130

E

Edit menu, 14
    Replace command, 80
edit mode, 120
Edit Relationships dialog box, 207
editing
    data, 64
    data access page, 242-244
    fields, 72
    information in forms, 134-135
    labels, 120-121
    queries, 166
    shortcuts, 77
    switching from navigation mode, 73
    undoing, 74-75
effects, reports, 196-199
entering
    data, 64
    information
        forms, 134-135
        tables, 66-69
Exit command (File menu), 33
exiting Access 2000, 33
Expedition option, 100
Export command (File menu), 218
Export Table To dialog box, 218
Export Text Wizard dialog box, 220
exporting information, 218-221
**Expression Builder dialog box, 126,
195**

F

Field List button, 177, 214
Field Name column (fields), 44
fields
    adding
        in Datasheet view, 58
        in Design view, 44

forms, 99-105
pop-up tips, 128-129
queries, 148-151, 160
reports, 177
Yes/No, 48-49
Available Fields list, 99
calculated
adding, 124-127
queries, 161
reports, 192-195
changing
names, 52-53
order, 136-137
columns
Data Type, 44
Description, 45
Field Name, 44
deleting, 59
deselecting, 99
editing, 72
inserting, 56
labels, 186
moving, 118
forms, 106-107
reports, 188-191
within tables, 54
selecting, 99
File menu
Exit command, 33
Export command, 218
Import command, 222
Page Setup command, 200
Print command, 203
File New Database dialog box, 36
files. See databases
Fill/Back Color button, 130, 199
Filter by Form button, 84
Filter By Selection button, 83
filtering by form, 83-84
Find and Replace dialog box, 76
Find button, 76
Find Next button, 77-81
Find What text box (Find and Replace dialog box), 77-78
finding. See searching

Finish button, 101, 115, 174
folders
adding to databases, 36-37
Samples, 12
Font Size button, 178
footers, 108
Form Design View window, 102
Form Footer bar, 124
Form Header/Footer command (View menu), 108
Form Name text box, 132
Form Wizard, 98-99
Format menu
Freeze Columns command, 90
Hide Columns command, 92
Theme command, 245
Unhide Columns command, 93
forms. See also database forms
color, changing, 130-131
database, implementing, 94
Detail area, 104
fields
adding, 104-105
moving in design view, 106-107
filtering, 84
information, editing, 134-135
opening, 133
saving, 132
Forms button, 232
Forms object button, 17, 98, 133
Forms tab (Database window), 102
Forward button, 22
Freeze Columns command
Format menu, 90
shortcut menu, 91
freezing columns, 90

G-H

getting help, 20-26
Answer Wizard, 24
Contents, 20
context-sensitive help, 23
index, 26
Office Assistant, 30-31

group grid, 183
grouping records, 182-183
headers, 108
help, 20-21
accessing, 20
Answer Wizard, 20, 24
contents, 20
Contents tab button, 21
context-sensitive, 23
Hyperlinks, 22
index, 20, 26
Internet, 32
navigating, 22
Office Assistant, 20-31
asking questions, 30-31
choosing, 28-29
customizing, 29
dialog balloon, 30
online, 20
searching, 25
topics, 26
What's This option, 23
Help menu, 20
What's This command, 23
Help toolbar, 20
help window, 20
Hide Columns command (Format menu), 92
hiding columns, 92
Hyperlinks, help, 22

I-L

implementing database forms, 94
Import command (File menu), 222
Import Text Wizard dialog box, 223
importing information, 222-225
In a New Table button, 224
Index tab button (Help window), 26
indexes, 136
help, 26

information
   exporting, 218-221
   forms, editing, 134-135
   importing, 222-225
   replacing selected, 80-81
   retrieving from database. See queries
   searching for, 76-79
Insert menu
   Date and Time command, 180
   Page Numbers command, 180
   Subdatasheet command, 236
inserting fields, 56
Install Now button, 7
installing Access 2000, 4, 6
Internet, Access 2000 help, 32

Justified option, 100

Label button, 110, 178, 192, 215
labels
   creating, 110
   editing, 120-121
   moving on reports, 186-187
Large Icons button, 16
light bulb button, 20
List Box button, 116
list boxes, 116-117
List toolbar button, 16
Lookup tab (Field Properties pane), 49

M

Margins tab (Page Setup dialog box), 201
Matching Cases (Find and Replace dialog box), 78
menus
   commands, 14-15
   Edit, 14
   View, 15
Microsoft Web site, 32
Modify the table design button, 43
More button, 77
moving
   fields, 118

   form design view, 106-107
   labels, 186-187
   reports, 188-191
   within tables, 54
objects, 118

N

Name AutoCorrect, 230, 233
names (fields), changing, 52-53
navigating
   help, 22
   switching to editing mode, 73
New button, 98, 176
New Form dialog box, 98
New Object button, 96
New Query dialog box, 148
New Record button, 134
New Table dialog box, 60
Next button, 5, 42, 100
No button, 55, 97
No Primary Key button, 225
number fields, adding, 46-47

O

object buttons, choosing, 17
objects
   moving, 118
   Reports, 212
   selecting, 18-19, 119
Office Assistant, 20-31
   asking questions, 30-31
   choosing, 28-29
   customizing, 29
   dialog balloon, 30
Office Assistant dialog box, 29
OK button, 37, 132
online help, 20
Open button, 13, 51
Open the page button, 240
opening
   databases, 10-13

   forms, 133
   Query Design view, 142
   reports, 176
   tables, 51
   windows, Form Design View, 102
option buttons, 122-123
options
   Expedition, 100
   Form Wizard (New Form dialog box), 98
   Justified, 100
Options tab (Office Assistant dialog box), 29
OR criteria, 154-155
Other tab (property sheet), 136

P-Q

Page Footer bar, 215
page numbers, adding automatically, 180
Page Numbers command (Insert menu), 180
Page Numbers dialog box, 180
Page Setup command (File menu), 200
Page Setup dialog box, 200
pages
   data, 242-243
   titles, 178-179
Pages button, 238, 242
Paste button, 181
Personal button, 40
pop-up tips, adding, 128-129
Primary Key button, 62
primary toolbar, 16
Print button, 203
Print command (File menu), 203
Print dialog box, 203
printing reports, 203
properties
   ControlTip Text, 128
   Tab Stop, 137
Properties button, 125